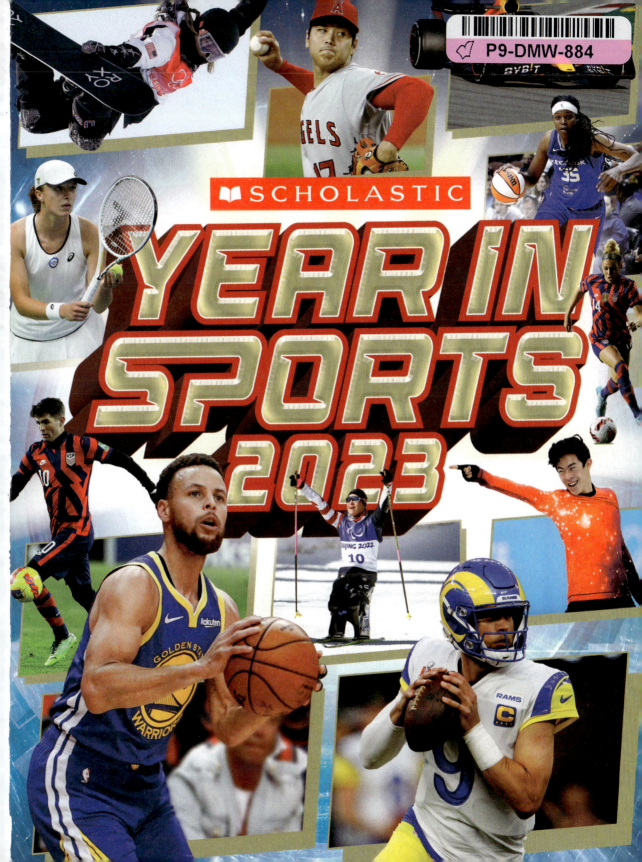

SCHOLASTIC

YEAR IN SPORTS 2023

ISBN 978-1-338-84751-2

10 9 8 7 6 5 4   23 24 25 26

Printed in the U.S.A.   40
First edition, December 2022

Produced by Shoreline Publishing Group LLC

Due to the publication date, records, results, and statistics are current as of mid-August 2022.

Contents

Back in Action!

Hello, sports fans! Welcome back to the field/arena/gym/pool/track, etc. While COVID-19 still plays a part in our world, the past sports season was (mostly) back to normal. Thank goodness! What would we do without our favorite sports?! As always, COVID or no COVID, the YEAR IN SPORTS is here to help you recap and remember the past 365 days of amazing action from sports around the world.

The biggest event on the past year's calendar happened in China, when 2022 Winter Olympic Games athletes skied, skated, and sledded onto your screens. American snowboarders were once again dominant (we're looking at you, **Chloe Kim**!), but new stars emerged as well. Check out all the action in our story on the Games beginning on page 18.

Women's sports continued to gain more attention as amazing athletes got big piles of TV time. The WNBA had some of its best ratings ever, along with some of its best action—and a surprise champion! The US women's soccer team continued its dominance and set itself up for a big 2023, when the World Cup comes around again. Speaking of soccer, the men's World Cup will be played after we print this book, but on page 140, we've got a fun way for you to record the action as you root for the United States (and, of course, your other favorite countries!).

Chloe Kim flashes a gold-medal smile!

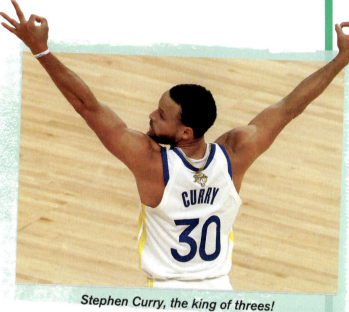

Stephen Curry, the king of threes!

As usual, the "Big Four" American sports provided thrills aplenty. Baseball fans were shocked to see the Atlanta Braves win the World Series. Football fans saw another title from Alabama, and also a big home-field win from the Los Angeles Rams in the Super Bowl. Hockey saw a new champion emerge—find out who on page 116. In the NBA, **Stephen Curry** and the Golden State Warriors returned to the top, continuing a run of greatness that started in 2015. Along the way, Curry became the league's all-time three-point champ!

Sports, of course, is way more than America! Soccer fans looked to Europe in 2022 to see a new women's champion and familiar Champions League winners. Formula 1 fans enjoyed the closest finish in the history of that fast-moving supersport. Inside, you'll also meet tennis champs from around the world, golfing heroes from three continents, and the Tour de France winners.

For the first time, we are also featuring the Special Olympics, held every four years to bring athletes of all abilities together to show off their hard work and talent. They're every bit as awesome as Kim, Curry, and **Cooper Kupp**!

So find a comfy chair, or gather up a team of pals, and get ready to dive into another action-packed year of sports. Don't worry, we're already watching and taking notes for *next year's* big book! Thanks for reading!

MOMENTS IN SPORTS
SEPTEMBER 2021–AUGUST 2022

The sports world (and almost everyone else) breathed a big sigh of relief as things got back to (mostly) normal in late 2021. The World Series was played, the whole NFL season made it through, the Winter Olympics squeaked in during early 2022, and the WNBA, NBA, and NHL seasons reached their ends. Why the relief? COVID was (again . . . mostly!) not a barrier to fans watching and enjoying sports. We're not all done with the pandemic yet, of course, but this past year had a long list of memorable moments. Here is our choice for the Top Ten. If it's not the same as yours, well . . . that's the great thing about sports!

10 **NFL INSTANT CLASSIC** *How wild was the AFC playoff game between Kansas City and Buffalo? So wild that it led to a change in NFL rules! The awesome back-and-forth battle saw two young superstar QBs—***Patrick Mahomes** *of the Chiefs (pictured) and* **Josh Allen** *of the Bills—lead their teams on late drive after late drive. The Bills scored twice in the last two minutes, but Mahomes had enough time for the Chiefs to tie. The Chiefs got the ball first in OT, drove for a TD, and won. All Buffalo could do was watch. The rule change? Starting in the 2022 season, playoff OT rules were changed to give each team a chance.*

9 FORMULA 1 FINISH

Formula 1 has recently rocketed to big US fame, thanks in part to a streaming documentary series. All those new fans were treated to the closest finish in the series' long history. Seven-time champ **Lewis Hamilton** *and rising star* **Max Verstappen** *battled to the last lap of the last race. With Hamilton ahead, a strange decision by F1 officials to send out a safety car let Verstappen catch and pass the champ on one of the final turns. They will be talking about this finish for a long time.*

8 **ATLANTA SURPRISE** *On June 16, 2021, the Atlanta Braves were five games under .500. Their chance at a World Series win seemed dim. They rallied and made the playoffs, but still, their 88 wins were the fewest of any of the 10 MLB playoff teams. Somehow, they beat the Milwaukee Brewers and the highly favored Los Angeles Dodgers. In the World Series, they used great pitching from young stars* **Max Fried** *and* **Ian Anderson**, *and clutch hitting from slugger* **Freddie Freeman** *to beat the Houston Astros in six games. Surprise!*

7 **GOLDEN CHLOE** *When **Chloe Kim** won the 2018 snowboard halfpipe gold medal at the Winter Olympics, she was only 17. By the time the 2022 Winter Games rolled around, she was a "veteran," but still just 21! She used her experience and high-flying skills to win a second consecutive gold in her specialty. The young American star became the first woman ever to go back-to-back in the event.*

6

UPSETS AND COMEBACKS *Fans depend on the NCAA basketball tournaments to provide thrills and chills. The 2022 events were no disappointment. The women's champion was not a big surprise—South Carolina won wire-to-wire. On the men's side, though, No. 15–seed St. Peter's shocked No. 2–seed Kentucky in a huge upset. St. Peter's later became the first No. 15 seed to make it to the Elite Eight. After winning an instant classic over Duke in the semifinal, North Carolina led Kansas by 15 points at halftime. But Kansas capped a wild tournament by coming from behind to win!*

5 HOME RUN HERO *Jocelyn Alo* grew up in Hawaii dreaming of becoming a big-time softball star. She worked hard, hitting 1,000 pitches a day in her backyard. After joining the Oklahoma Sooners, she made her dream come true. In March 2022, she hit her 96th career home run—in front of her hometown fans in Hawaii, no less!—setting a new NCAA record. She kept slugging and finished her four-year Sooners career with 122 longballs. She also helped her school win back-to-back national championships!

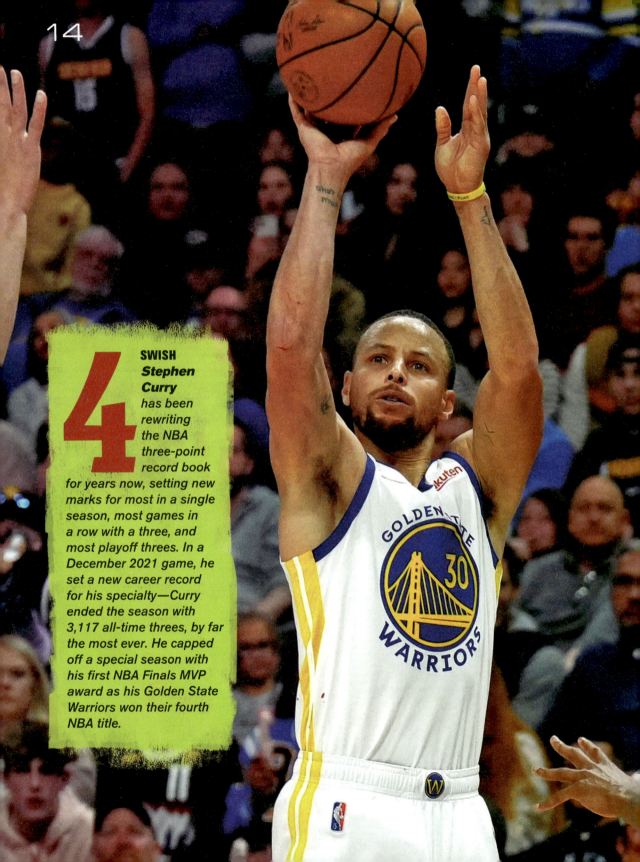

4

SWISH *Stephen Curry* has been rewriting the NBA three-point record book for years now, setting new marks for most in a single season, most games in a row with a three, and most playoff threes. In a December 2021 game, he set a new career record for his specialty—Curry ended the season with 3,117 all-time threes, by far the most ever. He capped off a special season with his first NBA Finals MVP award as his Golden State Warriors won their fourth NBA title.

3

MR. EVERYTHING *The Los Angeles Angels had two of the best players in baseball in 2021—and both were the same guy!* **Shohei Ohtani** *had a season for the ages, winning the AL MVP after smacking 46 homers, stealing 26 bases, and oh, yes, also winning nine games as a pitcher with a 3.18 ERA! He kept it up in 2022—in one game, he hit a 446-foot homer while racking up 8 RBI; in the next, he struck out a career-best 13 batters! What's next for Ohtani . . . winning a Super Bowl?*

2

RAM TOUGH *The Los Angeles Rams traded for QB **Matthew Stafford** before the 2021 season. They added veteran LB **Von Miller**. They built up a team aimed at one goal: winning the Super Bowl, which would be played in their home SoFi Stadium. No team had ever done that, but the Rams made it happen. WR **Cooper Kupp** had one of the best seasons ever, while Miller teamed with defensive star **Aaron Donald**. The Rams beat the Cincinnati Bengals 23-20 in Super Bowl LVI to set off a Southern California party!*

1

AMERICAN GOLD *Nathan Chen* already had a room full of medals and trophies. The Utah native was a six-time US champion and a three-time world champion. The one thing he was missing from his amazing career was a Winter Olympics gold. He had fallen at the 2018 Games and didn't medal. But he stuck with it, kept training and improving, and dominated at the 2022 Games in China. He set a world record in the short program, then landed five quad jumps in the free skate. Finally . . . Nathan got his gold!

2022 WINTER OLYMPICS

UP, UP, AND AWAY!
American snowboarder Chloe Kim celebrates after soaring above the halfpipe at the 2022 Winter Olympics in China. Kim had earned her second gold medal in the event—the first woman ever to go back-to-back. Her success was just one part of a Winter Games packed with gold-medal stories, surprise winners, and new records. Put on your mittens and start reading!

The colorful Opening Ceremonies included these dancers waving LED sticks to look like a field of grass.

2022 Winter Olympics

How do you hold a Winter Olympic Games without snow? Simple—you make it yourself! China hosted the 2022 Winter Games, but that nation doesn't get nearly as much snow as other countries that have held the Games. Indoor ice events were easy; they were held in arenas with ice rinks. Outdoors, though, the organizers used snow cannons and machines to make snow! They covered frozen hillsides with ribbons of the white stuff, forming skiing runs, snowboard pipes, and cross-country tracks. Once the Olympians got used to it, it was just like Mother Nature's version.

Mother Nature did play a big part in the Games, though. On several days, the weather turned bitter cold. Some cross-country skiing events were shortened to protect the athletes. Still, some had to be treated for frostbite because of the sharp winds and low temperatures. At a few freestyle skiing and snowboarding events, the winds were so strong that athletes had to time their runs between gusts.

As if making snow was not a big enough deal, China had to deal with COVID-19. To protect the athletes, writers, TV personnel, and volunteers, the country pretty much locked the Olympic family into a bubble. Everyone was tested every day. No one could leave the Olympic areas. Writers sped in buses past tourist sites and tasty-looking restaurants. At most event sites, fans were not allowed to watch, either. Athletes feared a positive test would cause them to miss their event. While a few cases snuck in, the bubble pretty much worked. COVID didn't shut down the Games as some people had worried.

Some people still objected to having the Games in China. The country does not have the best record in human rights. Still, once the events began, the athletes focused on winning and not on politics.

With the snow made and the tests taken, it was time for the action! One of the big stories concerned Norway. Though the country has only 5.5 million people, it dominated the Winter Games for the second time in a row. Norwegian athletes won 16 gold medals, an all-time record for one country at a single Games. They won golds in six different sports. The home country, China, won eight gold medals. That's the most it has ever won at a Winter Olympics.

The American team did very well, too. **Chloe Kim** repeated as the women's snowboard halfpipe champion. Bobsledder **Elana Meyers Taylor** reached five career Winter medals. That's the most ever by a

Black athlete. **Nathan Chen** finally won gold in figure skating. After earning several World Championships, this was his first Olympic win. And US skiers crushed the freestyle events. Eight of the country's 25 medals came in that one sport!

From the ice rinks to the ski slopes, from the bobsled run to the halfpipe, the Winter Games were packed with awesome action. Read on to relive the biggest moments!

FINAL MEDAL STANDINGS

COUNTRY	G	S	B	TOTAL
1. **Norway**	16	8	13	37
2. **ROC***	6	12	14	32
3. **Germany**	12	10	5	27
4. **Canada**	4	8	14	26
5. **United States**	8	10	7	25
6. **Sweden**	8	5	5	18
7. **Austria**	7	7	4	18
8. **Japan**	3	6	9	18
9. **Netherlands**	8	5	4	17
10. **Italy**	2	7	8	17

*Russian Olympic Committee

Olympic workers spend a lot of time grooming the snow.

"I'm so grateful for [my parents]—I feel like this is the least I could do for how much they've done for me. It pushes me to work harder than ever before."

— CHLOE KIM

Figure Skating

MEN'S SINGLES

Nathan Chen had won six US championships and three World Championships. But he missed out on an Olympic medal back in 2018. Ever since, he had aimed at this event in 2022, and he came through like a champ. Chen set a world record with 113.97 points in the short program. Three Japanese skaters, including defending champ **Yuzuru Hanyu**, were trailing him.

In the free skate final, Chen made every move almost perfectly. He landed five "quads," which are flying spins in which he rotates four times! His score of 332.60 was enough to win the gold. Chen's parents were born in China before moving to the United States, and he was born in Salt Lake City, Utah. "I know that they did everything that they could to give all of us–I'm the youngest of five–the opportunities to pursue [our dreams]," he said. Chen was the first American man to win gold since **Evan Lysacek** in 2010.

23 If you add up all of Nathan Chen's medals from international events, plus his six US national championships, you come up with this big number!

A Problem in Women's Singles

Russian star **Kamila Valieva** helped her country win gold in the team event. Then it was announced that she had tested positive for a banned substance back home. She should not have been allowed to continue, but a sports court said she could. It was shocking news. Figure skaters were very upset. Though Valieva should have known better, she was still just 15 and doing what her coaches said. So when she fell in the women's final and finished fourth, she was in tears. To make matters worse, her coach yelled at her. She had done wrong, but it was hard not to feel bad for her, too. Her teammate, **Anna Shcherbakova**, won the gold medal. American **Alysa Liu** finished seventh.

Valieva after her final skate

SKATING NOTES

✳ The American team earned a surprise silver medal in the team event. **Nathan Chen** had a great short program to pile up points. **Karen Chen** (no relation to Nathan) followed the next day with a solid performance. And near the end of the event, **Madison Chock** and **Evan Bates** won the ice dance section to push the United States into second place overall.

✳ In the ice dance medal event, the French team of **Gabriella Papadakis** and **Guillaume Cizeron** thrilled fans with a beautiful gold-medal-winning performance. Americans

Madison Hubbell and **Zachary Donohue** won bronze, while Chock and Bates finished fourth.

✳ Hometown heroes **Sui Wenjing** and **Han Cong** of China won the pairs event. Their score was just 63 hundredths ahead of the second-place team. They had earned silver in the 2018 Games.

Donohue and Hubbell brought home a medal.

Skiing

Shiffrin Shocker: The biggest news in these events was what didn't happen. American star **Mikaela Shiffrin** (right), one of the best skiers of all time, had her eye on medals in all five of her individual events. But in the slalom and giant slalom early in the Games, she made shocking mistakes and could not finish either race. Fans around the country watched her tears as she tried to recover. She finished ninth in the Super-G and then ran into trouble again in the combined event, missing a gate in the slalom part. She finished her downhill run but wasn't fast enough for a medal. In the team event, she did well, but the US team finished fourth. She was sad after the Games, but it just shows that even the greatest champions can hit a bad patch.

Family Story: **Ryan Cochran-Siegle** has been living with an Olympic champion his whole life. His mother, Barbara, won a slalom gold in 1972. Her three siblings also made the Games. Ryan learned to ski on the family's small ski mountain in Vermont. In 2021, he suffered a broken neck in a bad crash, but battled back to make it to China. In the Super-G, he finished second by only 0.04 seconds to earn a silver medal. He said earning the medal was "a childhood dream." Now there's another medal for the Cochran house to hang!

Cross Country/Biathlon Notes

➔ **Marte Olsbu Røiseland** was the star of the biathlon competition. She helped Norway win the mixed-team relay event and got a bronze in the 15 km race. She earned her second gold in the 7.5 km sprint, and then made it three golds for her in China with a 10 km pursuit victory. The men's star was France's **Quentin Fillon Maillet**. He won two golds and three silvers.

➔ In cross-country, the ROC's **Alexander Bolshunov** shrugged off the bitter cold and won five medals, including three golds. **Jessie Diggins** became the first American woman with multiple medals. She earned bronze in the sprint freestyle and silver in the 30 km race.

Diggins made US skiing history!

SKIING NOTES

✳ The men's downhill was won by 34-year-old **Beat Feuz** of Switzerland, the oldest skiing gold medalist ever. Silver medalist **Johan Clarey** of France was even older at 41!

✳ Austria's **Matthias Mayer** continued his winning streak. After earning gold medals in 2014 and 2018, he added the Super-G gold and downhill bronze in China.

✳ **Michelle Gisin** of Switzerland had a great Games. She won the combined event and finished third in Super-G.

◀ Austria's **Johannes Strolz** sped to victory in the combined event (a mix of downhill and slalom races). His father, Hubert, won gold in the same event in 1988, making them the first-ever parent and child to win the same event at the Winter Olympics.

Freestyle Skiing

Alex Hall

Eight of the 25 medals won by Americans at these Games were for freestyle skiing, the most in any sport!

Top Team-Up

After other athletes saw what **Alex Hall** did in the slopestyle event, they were in shock. "He looks like he just ignores gravity," said a TV commentator. Hall's score of 90.01 was good for gold. His teammate **Nick Goepper** earned the silver, a medal he had also won in 2018.

Teaming Up for Gold

This Games introduced a new sport, mixed team aerials. The scores by high-flying male and female skiers were added up to find a winner.

China was expected to win big, but in an upset, the American team of **Ashley Caldwell**, **Christopher Lillis**, and **Justin Schoenefeld** piled up enough points to carry home the gold.

Two-Three in Halfpipe

New Zealand's **Nico Porteous** added to a great Games for the far-away island nation. He won gold in the halfpipe. He finished

Gu shows off her medals.

GU FOR GOLD

Eileen Gu was one of the biggest winners at these Games. She won two gold medals in freestyle skiing events: halfpipe and Big Air. She also got a silver in slopestyle. Fans on both sides of the Pacific Ocean were cheering for her. Gu was representing China, but she was born in and grew up in the US. She chose to race for China to help promote winter sports in the land where her mother was born.

Colby Stevenson gets Big Air!

just ahead of Americans **David Wise** and **Alex Ferreira**.

Medals All Around

In the men's Big Air event, Norway's **Birk Ruud** won, but American Colby Stevenson was the big story, earning a silver medal. **Stevenson** had been in a bad car accident in 2016. He had to battle back from broken bones, a damaged skull, and other injuries. It took him months of work with doctors. Seeing him soar to success was one of the Games' most inspiring stories. Plus, American skier **Megan Nick** landed in third in the Aerials event, while **Jaelin Kauf** won silver in women's Moguls.

BEIJING 2022

David Wise was all smiles when he won silver!

Snowboarders and judges alike went wild for Ayumu Hirano's spectacular spins!

Snowboarding

HALFPIPE

Men

Shaun White is probably the most famous snowboarder of all time. He won three gold medals in halfpipe, including a surprising comeback win in 2018. He said before these Games began that these would be his last. And he almost added another medal, coming in fourth to end his great career. Japan's **Ayumu Hirano** blew away the judges in the final to win gold. He performed three triple corks, the first time that trick had ever been done in an Olympic final. Australia's **Scotty James** took

Goodbye to Shaun White!

silver, and **Jan Scherrer** of Switzerland earned the bronze ahead of White.

Women

Winning one gold medal is pretty awesome. Coming back four years later is even more amazing! Everyone is aiming to knock you off the top spot, and you have to work extra hard to defend your title. But **Chloe Kim** came up with the right plan. In her first run down the halfpipe in the medal run, she did flips and spins and grabs that piled up 94.0 points. No one else came close in round after round. She became the first woman ever to go back-to-back in this event.

Winner! Jacobellis slides through in first!

SNOWBOARD NOTES

✳ **Julia Marino** of the US team won a silver in the women's slopestyle event.

✳ **Ester Ledecká** of the Czech Republic repeated as the gold medalist in the women's parallel giant slalom.

✳ Canada's **Max Parrot** was a double medalist. He earned bronze in the men's Big Air event, and captured gold in slopestyle.

SNOWBOARD CROSS

This high-speed, high-action racing sport thrilled fans at home thanks to superstar snowboarder **Lindsey Jacobellis**. The US star had won just about every World Cup and national title she could, but still had no Olympic gold, though she had come close. In the women's final, she raced past France's **Chloé Trespeuch** early in the race and held on for the win. In the team event, she made it two golds in a row. In this event, a male and female racer each take a run. **Nick Baumgartner** won his part and Jacobellis followed with another great ride to win the gold. With a combined age of 76, they were the oldest pair in the event, and the 40-year-old Baumgartner became the oldest snowboarder to win an Olympic medal.

Around the Games

O Canada! A happy team of women's hockey players celebrates their gold.

WOMEN'S HOCKEY

Everyone knew who would play in the gold-medal game. It just had to be the United States and Canada. The two countries have won every Olympic gold medal ever awarded in this sport. They have faced off in the World Championships another 18 times. The US team lost key forward **Brianna Decker** to an injury in the first round. But they kept battling and kept scoring. They beat Finland in the semifinals to set up the expected gold-medal match.

The game didn't go the Americans' way. They fell behind 3-1 after two periods. They managed a final goal in the last minute, but it was not enough. The Canadians celebrated on the ice after winning their fifth gold in the sport, which started in the Games in 1998.

MEN'S HOCKEY

The National Hockey League did not let its players take part in these Winter Games. So the American team was built with college players, minor leaguers, and former pros. They surprised many with success. In group play, the team beat China and Germany, and defeated Canada, usually a tough foe, 4-2. In the quarterfinal, the US team led Slovakia with a minute left, but gave up a tying goal. After no one scored in overtime, Slovakia won in a shootout, knocking the United States out of the medals. Finland won its first Olympic title.

BOBSLED

A new event joined the "sliding" sports for this Olympics. In monobob, only a single rider steers a bobsled down the twisting course. In the event, Americans finished first and second, with **Kaillie Humphries** getting the gold and **Elana Meyers Taylor** the silver. In the two-man event, Germany had an Olympic bobsled first by earning gold, silver, and bronze. Meyers Taylor teamed with **Sylvia Hoffman** to bronze in the two-woman race.

LUGE

Along with lots of bobsled success, German athletes "owned" the luge. **Johannes Ludwig** won the men's singles, while **Natalie Geisenberger** won the women's. **Anna Berreiter** earned a silver for Germany, too. **Tobias Arlt** and **Tobias Wendl** won the men's doubles (Germany got silver there, too!). And take one guess what nation won the team relay event! Germany also won both golds in the skeleton races. (In these races, the sledders go down headfirst!)

Meyers Taylor earned two medals in '22.

A FULL SET

Coming into these Games, Sweden's **Niklas Edin** had an empty spot in his trophy case. He had a curling bronze medal from 2014 and a silver for 2018. In 2022, he made the set complete, leading Sweden to its first Olympic title. Sweden beat Great Britain in the final, while Canada squeaked past the United States to earn the bronze.

More Around the Games

SPEEDSKATING

FAMOUS FIRST: Erin Jackson (right) became the first Black American woman with a speedskating medal when she won the 500 meters. She finished ahead of Japan's **Miho Takagi** by only 8 hundredths of a second! It was also the first US win in this event since 1994. Jackson almost didn't reach these Games after slipping in the Olympic Trials. But teammate **Brittany Bowe** gave Jackson, a World Cup champion, her spot, and Jackson made the most of it! And Bowe also earned a bronze in the 1000-meter race!

SUPER SWEDE: Sweden's **Nils van der Poel** made headlines for the men. He won gold in the 5,000 meters and in the 10,000 meters; in the second event, he set a new world record!

Schouten earning one of her four medals

DUTCH DOMINATION: The Netherlands has won most of the speedskating medals in recent Olympics. **Irene Schouten** kept that streak going with gold in the women's 3,000- and 5,000-meter races. She also won the mass start gold and a bronze in team pursuit. Her teammate **Ireen Wüst** earned her sixth career gold with a win in the 1,500 meters. She also set a record by becoming the first person to win a gold medal in five different Olympics! At 35, she is also the oldest speedskating gold medalist ever.

Paralympics

A few days after the Winter Games ended—and while the world watched Russia invade Ukraine (page 34)—another amazing group of athletes took to the ice and snow in China in a quest for medals. The Winter Paralympics were held in China for the first time in 2022, and the host country made the most of them. China led the way in the medal count with 61 overall, including a surprising bronze in sled hockey and its second straight gold in wheelchair curling.

One of the biggest stories of the Games was the continued success of American athlete **Oksana Masters**. With a total of seven medals in Beijing, including three golds, she became the all-time leader in Paralympic medals by an American with 14. She's a cross-country and biathlon skier in winter, and she's also a star cyclist and rower in the Summer Games, where she has won three more medals!

Another medals champ was **Brian McKeever**. The Canadian tied the all-time record for Paralympic golds with his 16th victory in cross-country skiing for the visually impaired. He won all three of his races at a Paralympics for the fourth time.

American athletes performed very well at these Paralympics, the eleventh ever held. US stars won 20 medals! A highlight was the fourth straight gold for the men's hockey team, which they earned with a 5-0 win over rival Canada. **Brenna Huckaby** repeated her gold in banked slalom. Canada's team posted 25 medals to come in third, its second-best showing in Winter Paralympics history.

Masters was the Paralympics master!

FINAL MEDAL STANDINGS

COUNTRY	G	S	B	TOTAL
1. China	18	20	23	61
2. Ukraine	11	10	8	29
3. Canada	8	6	11	25
4. United States	6	11	3	20
5. Germany	4	8	7	19
6. Austria	5	5	3	13
7. France	7	3	2	12

More Paralympics

Gretsch completed an Olympic double.

Double Gold

Kendall Gretsch wrapped up a rare Olympic double when she captured gold in the sprint sitting biathlon. Gretsch had also won a gold medal in the triathlon at the Summer Olympics in 2021!

Daughter Day!

In some alpine skiing events for the visually impaired, the athletes ski with guides. The two act as a team and need to train for many months. But the guide for Belgium's **Linda Le Bon** was not able to travel due to COVID. So at the last minute, **Ulla Gilot**, Le Bon's daughter, jumped onto her skis and helped her mom finish sixth in the Super-G.

INSPIRATION

These Games began just weeks after Russia invaded Ukraine. The Russian athletes were not allowed to take part as a punishment for their government's actions. The athletes from Ukraine tried to carry on even as their friends and family back home suffered in the war. The athletes did more than that—they were inspired, setting a new record for their nation with 29 medals, the second-most behind China. Ukrainian athletes even swept two biathlon events, one each for men and women. **Oksana Masters** of the US team, who was born in Ukraine, said she was donating all her prize money to help physically impaired kids in Ukraine.

Biathlon silver medalist Oleksandra Kononova

Momoka Muraoka shows how Paralympics skiers use one ski plus two poles with runners.

Fabulous Family

A trio of **Aigners** from Austria will need to build a very big family trophy case. **Johannes** won two golds, two silvers, and a bronze in visually impaired alpine events. Not bad for a 16-year-old! His sisters did pretty well, too. Also racing in visually impaired events, **Veronika** won two golds, while **Barbara** earned a silver and a bronze, twice finishing just behind her sister! Bonus points for **Elisabeth**, who acted as a guide for Veronika.

British First

Great Britain claimed its first-ever gold medal at the Winter Paralympics. Since the idea of adaptive sports started in that country back in the 1940s, that made **Neil Simpson**'s win in Super-G vision impaired that much sweeter. His brother **Andrew** served as his guide in the winning race.

Marvelous Momoka

Japan's **Momoka Muraoka** sped to three gold medals in sitting skiing events. She won the downhill, Super-G, and giant slalom, and she was second in the super combined. Her four medals in one Games were a first for Japan. The medals increase her career total to nine, among the most ever by an athlete from Japan.

Johannes Aigner (left) and his guide skied to gold.

A NEW KIND OF DOUBLE PLAY
The biggest story of the 2021 Major League Baseball season was the two-way success of Shohei Ohtani. The Japanese superstar was one of the best hitters in the game . . . and he was also one of the best pitchers! Read more about him on page 42, plus relive lots of great memories from the 2021 season. Play ball!

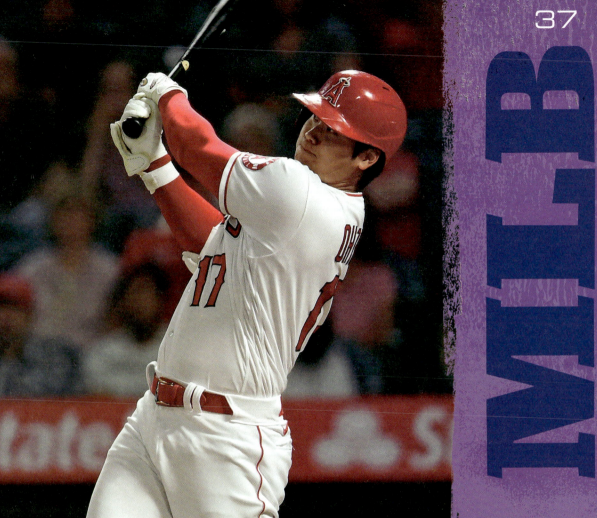

MLB

Play Ball, 2021 Style!

Play ball! Those were the best words that baseball fans heard in 2021, mostly because they heard them in person! COVID rules relaxed enough so that most ballparks were able to welcome back some fans. By the summer, stadiums were packed. Those fans saw some great baseball, some surprising results, and some new heroes.

The biggest story of the season was probably the incredible two-way success of Angels pitcher/DH **Shohei Ohtani**. For more on his Babe Ruthian season, see page 42.

Another big story was on the mound. Some pitchers got in trouble early for using illegal sticky stuff to make their pitches move. MLB started new rules to inspect pitchers, and some pretty good pitchers were suddenly just average. Still, pitchers had some pretty good days, with a new record of nine no-hitters being pitched (see page 43).

As the season got underway, all the experts predicted a sad one for the San Francisco Giants. Some computers picked SF to only win 78 games. Shows how much the experts know! The Giants led the National League in homers, had one of the best pitching staffs, and led the way at the end with 107 wins. That was an all-time record for a team that began back in 1883!

Jacob deGrom

On the other side of the W-L line, the Arizona Diamondbacks put together a streak to forget. They started out 23–63, including a long 17-game losing streak.

The Mets' ace **Jacob deGrom** had a hot start of his own. He put together one of the best first halves in MLB history. He struck out 103 in his first 10 games, covering 64 innings. After 12 starts, his ERA was a minuscule 0.50. At one point, he had more RBI with his bat than earned runs he had given up. Unfortunately, a sore elbow shut down his amazing season in July.

Speaking of midseason, fans needed lots of help to find their favorite players. More All-Star players were traded or changed teams before the trade deadline than ever before. The LA Dodgers picked up **Max Scherzer** and **Trea Turner**. The Yankees added sluggers **Anthony Rizzo** and **Joey Gallo**. Superstar **Javier Báez** became a NY Met, while Cubs hero **Kris Bryant** joined the surprising Giants. Toronto signed top closer **Brad Hand** and slugger **Nelson Cruz** became a Tampa Bay Ray.

Those new players helped their teams stay in the fight for playoff spots. As the regular season got close to the end, fans enjoyed some final thrills! The Chicago White Sox and Houston Astros clinched spots early, as did the Tampa Bay Rays. But in both leagues, deciding the playoff teams went down to the wire. The AL wild-card race came down to the last inning of the last game. At one point, four teams could have won or tied for the two wild-card spots. Toronto and Seattle had a shot if the Red Sox and Yankees lost. Toronto won and then had to wait. Seattle, meanwhile, got crushed by the Angels. That made it 20 years without playoffs for the Mariners, the longest streak currently among all major men's sports.

On the final Sunday, the Yankees won their game on a walk-off single by **Aaron**

Devers sent the Sox to the playoffs.

Judge to clinch a spot. Moments later, Boston's **Rafael Devers** smacked a two-run homer to give the Red Sox a win and the other wild-card spot, setting up a showdown at Fenway Park.

In the NL West, the Giants needed a win on the final day to clinch and keep the Dodgers from tying them. They came through over the Padres, even as the Dodgers won to keep pace. LA set a new MLB record for having the most wins as a second-place team, with 106. They were forced into a one-game wild-card playoff.

And that was just how the playoffs started! To see all the steps of the wild and woolly 2021 MLB postseason, turn to page 44.

Around the Bases

Here are some of the highlight moments of the 2021 regular season from around the Major Leagues.

Rookie Record:

White Sox rookie catcher **Seby Zavala** had played 17 MLB games but hadn't hit a homer yet. Then he knocked his first three career long balls . . . in the same game! His big blasts helped Chicago beat Cleveland 12-11. It was the first time ever that a player's first three dingers came in one game.

A Blue Record:

On May 26, **Joe West** umpired his 5,376 MLB game, the most in history. West started his career calling balls and strikes in 1976. He worked six World Series and called one no-hitter. Why "blue"? That's the nickname for any ump, after the color of their long-ago uniforms. West retired after the season.

What a day! Three homers for Zavala!

Streaking Schwarb:

While with the Washington Nationals in June, **Kyle Schwarber** went on one of the hottest homer streaks ever. He cracked 15 home runs in 17 games! He later moved to the Red Sox and finished the season with 32 homers.

10-K:

Strikeouts have been way up in recent seasons, as more players swing for the fences instead of trying to get base hits. Pitchers have taken advantage. In 2021, two hurlers did something that had only been done once before: strike out 10 batters in a row. First, in June, the Phillies' **Aaron Nola** sent 10 Mets back to the dugout. Then, in August, Milwaukee's **Corbin Burnes** (who went on to be the NL Cy Young winner) mowed down

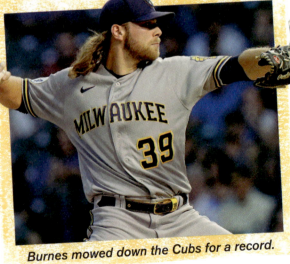

Burnes mowed down the Cubs for a record.

Cabrera added to his great career.

10 straight Cubs. Both tied a record set by **Tom Seaver** in 1970.

Miggy Mash: Detroit slugger **Miguel Cabrera** is certainly on his way to the Hall of Fame someday. He added another page to his great record book with his 500th career homer. The blast came in an August game. He was the 28th player to reach 500 in big-league history. What else has this great Tigers hero done? Back-to-back MVPs (2012 and 2013); the last Triple Crown in the Majors (2013; the only one since 1967); four batting titles; 11 All-Star Games. He got the 2022 season started off with a bang, too. In a game in April, he smacked his 3,000th career hit. He became only the seventh player ever with 500 homers and 3,000 hits!

SOMEWHERE IN IOWA

Have you seen the movie *Field of Dreams*? If you haven't, you should. It's a baseball classic. In the movie, a man has a dream that tells him to build a baseball diamond on his cornfield in Iowa. Then ghostly players from the past appear to play on it! There's lots more. The point is that the field really was built for the movie and it became a huge tourist attraction. For the first time, a Major League game was played on a field

nearby, and millions watched on TV while a lucky few watched in person. And it ended in a storybook way, with **Tim Anderson** of the White Sox smacking a walk-off two-run homer into the outfield cornstalks to beat the New York Yankees 9-8. Another Field of Dreams game was scheduled for 2022 after we printed this book.

Amazing Ohtani!

Almost since baseball began, pitchers pitched and hitters hit. Only a small number of players could do both well. One was the great **Babe Ruth**, who hit 714 homers but was also one of the AL's best pitchers for four seasons. No one had come close since—until 2021.

Since joining the Angels in 2018, **Shohei Ohtani** had shown that he could both pitch well and hit very well. However, injuries had kept him from doing both for a whole season. He was healthy in 2021, and the entire sports world enjoyed one of the greatest shows in baseball history.

Ohtani was the unanimous choice for the AL MVP after hitting 46 homers, stealing 26 bases, finishing tied for first with 8 triples, and putting up a .965 OPS, second-best in the league. Incredibly, he also made 23 starts on the mound and was almost as good there. He finished with a 9–2 record and a 3.18 ERA, while striking out 156–an average of 1.2 per inning.

Season of the No-No!

While home runs continued to fly out of the yard, the 2021 season was also a memorable one for pitchers. They teamed up to throw more no-hitters than in any season, surpassing the mark of eight set back in 1884! And that's the season in which pitchers were first allowed to throw overhand. Before that, baseball was played like softball, with fast underhand pitching. Highlights included a no-no in his first MLB start by Arizona's Tyler Gilbert and the first one in Padres history by Joe Musgrove. Here is the honor roll.

Spencer Turnbull

PITCHER, TEAM	SCORE, OPPONENT
Joe Musgrove, Padres	**3-0**, Rangers
Carlos Rodón, White Sox	**8-0**, Cleveland
John Means, Orioles	**6-0**, Mariners
Wade Miley, Reds	**3-0**, Cleveland
Spencer Turnbull, Tigers	**5-0**, Mariners
Corey Kluber, Yankees	**2-0**, Rangers
Combined*, Cubs	**4-0**, Dodgers
Tyler Gilbert, Diamondbacks	**7-0**, Padres
Combined*, Brewers	**3-0**, Cleveland

*The Cubs used four pitchers, while the Brewers' Corbin Burnes threw eight innings and Josh Hader the ninth.

CELEBRATE!

Several MLB teams created some memorable (and a little silly) home run celebrations. Here are some of them; which was your favorite?

Red Sox: The homer hitter was driven the length of the dugout in a laundry cart!

Blue Jays: A blue blazer covered with patches was ready for the hitter to wear.

Padres: Like some college football teams do after big plays, the hitter put on a huge, spinning necklace.

Phillies: Day or night, the homer hitter put on a big Phillies sun hat.

Rockies: Instead of a hat, Rockies players shared a huge pair of sunglasses.

Braves: Why not a hug from a panda? Pablo "Panda" Sandoval, that is.

MLB Playoffs

WILD-CARD GAMES

Dodgers 3, Cardinals 1

Chris Taylor hit a walk-off two-run homer to make sure the Dodgers' team-record-tying 106 wins didn't go to waste. The Cardinals had won 19 out of 20 games in September but fell short here.

Red Sox 6, Yankees 2

Baseball's best rivalry added another chapter. **Xander Bogaerts** hit a two-run homer in the first inning and later threw out **Aaron Judge** at home plate. Boston pitcher **Nathan Eovaldi** allowed only one run in five and one-third innings.

NLDS

Dodgers 3, Giants 2

No two teams in baseball history with this many combined regular-season victories had ever faced each other. The Dodgers had 106 on the season, the Giants had 107. So it made sense that it came down to a classic Game 5. Giants pitching shut out the powerful Dodgers in Games 1 and 3. LA sluggers led the way in Games 2 and 4. In Game 5, former MVP **Cody Bellinger**—who hit only .165 in the 2021 season—came through with an RBI single in the ninth. The Dodgers then sent out ace starter **Max Scherzer** to earn his first-ever save. He came through and the Dodgers danced.

Braves 3, Brewers 1

Longtime Braves hero **Freddie Freeman** came through again, breaking a 4-4 tie in Game 4 with an eighth-inning homer. In a series dominated by pitching, that homer gave Atlanta enough to win the game and the series. Braves closer **Will Smith** saved all three of Atlanta's wins, which came after the Brewers claimed Game 1.

Bellinger celebrates his big hit.

ALDS

Red Sox 3, Rays 1

The Red Sox earned walk-off wins in back-to-back games to wrap up the series. **Christian Vázquez** homered to win Game 3, and then **Kiké Hernández** continued his hot hitting with a game-winning sac fly in Game 4. Though they had won the most games in the AL, the Rays went home early.

Astros 3, White Sox 1

The Astros mostly overpowered the White Sox, outscoring them 25-18 (and the White Sox got 12 of those runs in their only win). Six different Astros had at least 3 RBI in the series, led by **Kyle Tucker**'s 7, including two home runs.

Álvarez's power led the Astros to the World Series.

NLCS

Braves 4, Dodgers 2

The Braves shocked the 106-win Dodgers and earned their first trip to the World Series since 1999. **Eddie Rosario** led the way with 14 hits in the NLCS, which equaled the most hits by any player, in any series, in MLB history. The Dodgers' bats were quiet as the Braves won the first two games. The Dodgers won Game 3 with a big comeback, thanks in part to a homer by Bellinger. After another Atlanta win, the Dodgers clubbed Atlanta in Game 5. But **Ian Anderson** and the Braves bullpen closed the door with a 4-2 Game 6 win.

ALCS

Astros 4, Red Sox 2

After the Astros won Game 1, Boston's bats woke up and led the way to a pair of wins. In Game 2, the Red Sox became the first team ever with a pair of grand slams in a playoff game (by **J. D. Martinez** and **Rafael Devers**). A 12-2 win in Game 3 featured Hernández, who had eight hits in the first three games. Game 4 was tight until Houston scored seven late runs. Boston's bats never woke up again; Houston held them to one run in the final two games. Houston's **Yordan Álvarez** earned the MVP award, setting an ALCS record with a .522 average.

2021 World Series

Talk about a surprise team. In the history of baseball, no team had entered a World Series having as many days in a season with a losing record as the Atlanta Braves.

Soler went yard to lead off the Series.

GAME 1 Braves 6, Astros 2

Atlanta's **Jorge Soler** led off the game with a homer, the first player in World Series history to start Game 1 that way. The Braves scored five runs in the first three innings and never looked back, surprising the hometown Astros. Houston star **José Altuve** struck out three times in a postseason game for the first time in his career!

GAME 2 Astros 7, Braves 2

This time it was the Astros getting off to a fast start. With the score tied 1-1, Houston scored four runs in the second inning, though without any hard-hit balls. Atlanta didn't help itself, making an error and throwing a wild pitch. Altuve homered for the Astros' final run. That gave him 22 career postseason homers, tied for second-most all-time.

GAME 3 Braves 2, Astros 0

Five Braves pitchers allowed only two hits. **Austin Riley** and **Travis d'Arnaud** had the RBI and Atlanta took a 2-1 lead in the series. Houston didn't get its first hit until the eighth inning. No team has thrown a no-hitter in the World Series since **Don Larsen** of the Yankees threw a perfect game in 1956.

GAME 4 Braves 3, Astros 2

Back-to-back seventh-inning homers by **Dansby Swanson** and Soler turned a Houston lead into the final score. **Eddie Rosario** made a key catch at the wall for the Braves, and **Will Smith** nailed down the save again. **Kyle Wright** was also great in relief for the Braves, who moved to within a game of their first World Series title since 1995.

GAME 5 Astros 9, Braves 5

Atlanta's **Adam Duvall** got things off to a big start with a first-inning grand slam. But Houston came back to tie the game. After **Freddie Freeman** smashed a long homer to give the Braves the lead, back came the Astros. Led by **Marwin Gonzalez**'s pinch-hit two-run single and catcher **Martin Maldonado**'s three RBI, they retook the lead and never gave it up, sending the Series back to Houston, where the Astros were 51–30 in the regular season.

GAME 6 Braves 7, Astros 0

That thunderclap you heard was Soler's three-run homer soaring into the night sky in Houston. The Braves' DH absolutely crushed a pitch that literally left Minute Maid Park, landing in the parking lot outside. The blow silenced the Astros-loving crowd and led the way to the Braves' first championship since 1995. Swanson and Freeman added homers of their own, while young pitching ace **Max Fried** pitched six 4-hit shutout innings for the big win.

Fried struck out six and walked none in his Game 6 start.

2021 MLB Awards

MVP
AL: Shohei Ohtani ANGELS
NL: Bryce Harper PHILLIES

CY YOUNG AWARD
AL: Robbie Ray BLUE JAYS
NL: Corbin Burnes BREWERS

ROOKIE OF THE YEAR
AL: Randy Arozarena RAYS
NL: Jonathan India REDS

MANAGER OF THE YEAR
AL: Kevin Cash RAYS
NL: Gabe Kapler GIANTS

HANK AARON AWARD
◄ **AL: Vladimir Guerrero Jr.**
BLUE JAYS
NL: Bryce Harper PHILLIES

ROBERTO CLEMENTE AWARD
Nelson Cruz RAYS

2021 Stat Leaders

AL Hitting Leaders

48 HR
Vladimir Guerrero Jr., Blue Jays
Salvador Perez, Royals

121 RBI
Salvador Perez, Royals

.319 BATTING AVERAGE
Yuli Gurriel, Astros

191 HITS
Bo Bichette, Blue Jays

40 STOLEN BASES
Whit Merrifield, Royals

AL Pitching Leaders

16 WINS
Gerrit Cole, Yankees

2.84 ERA
248 STRIKEOUTS
Robbie Ray, Blue Jays

38 SAVES
Liam Hendriks, White Sox

NL Hitting Leaders

42 HR
Fernando Tatis Jr., Padres

113 RBI
Adam Duvall, Marlins/Braves

195 HITS
.328 BATTING AVERAGE
32 STOLEN BASES
Trea Turner, Nationals/Dodgers

NL Pitching Leaders

20 WINS
Julio Urías, Dodgers

2.43 ERA
Corbin Burnes, Brewers

39 SAVES
Mark Melancon, Padres

247 STRIKEOUTS
Zack Wheeler, Phillies

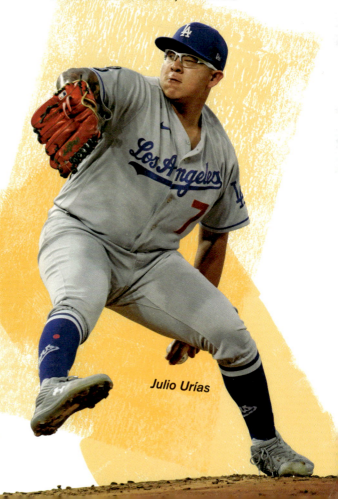

Julio Urías

NFL

SUPER RAMS!
The biggest NFL season ever ended with the biggest game . . . in one of the biggest stadiums! The Los Angeles Rams made a lot of hometown fans happy by winning Super Bowl LVI in their own SoFi Stadium. Led by wide receiver Cooper Kupp (right) and sackmaster Aaron Donald, the Rams beat the Cincinnati Bengals 23-20 in a thrilling end to a great 2021 NFL season. Read on!

The Biggest Season Ever!

You'll notice something new and different about the NFL standings (see box). If you add up each team's record, you'll reach 17 games. That's one more than teams played every season since 1978. In 2021, the NFL expanded to a 17-game season for the first time. Fans loved it, of course, because that meant six percent more football (do the math!). Owners loved it because it was one more stadium full of ticket buyers. Players were mixed: The extra game meant a bit more money, but it also meant another weekend of being tackled and blocked. But the plan worked well, with tight races in both conferences for playoff spots.

The biggest NFL season ever also included the most playoff teams. One team was added in each conference for a total of 14 in the playoffs. That also meant only one team would earn a bye with the overall best record. Just who that would be was a mystery for most of the season, as no team really broke out as a super-team in 2021. In the NFC, the Green Bay Packers clinched the top spot with a week to play, led by star QB **Aaron Rodgers**. In the AFC, the surprising Tennessee Titans were No. 1, thanks in part to running back **Derrick Henry**. However, Henry missed nine games and the Titans had five losses overall, so the AFC playoffs were wide open.

Below the top spots, new players made big impacts on their teams. The Los Angeles Rams traded for former Lions star **Matthew Stafford**. He's a big, powerful passer who was looking to join a winner. He led his new team to the NFC West title and a spot in the Super

Bengals WR Ja'Marr Chase

Bowl. The Cincinnati Bengals had a solid young offense, led by QB **Joe Burrow** and RB **Joe Mixon**, but they added pass-rushing star **Trey Hendrickson** and won their first division title since 2015. The Bengals also had the breakout rookie star of the year. WR **Ja'Marr Chase** set NFL rookie records with 1,429 receiving yards for the season and 266 yards in a game (in Week 17). With all those top players, the Bengals won their first playoff game in 31 years!

COVID-19 continued to affect the NFL, as it did everywhere. Most teams lost players due to testing or infection. A handful of games were rescheduled, too. In the end, however, every team played all of its 17 games.

Once the postseason began, fans settled in for some of the most exciting football of the season, including incredible comebacks, last-second field goals, and eye-popping catches. Read on to relive the biggest (and best?) NFL season ever!

Henry led the Titans to the top AFC mark.

2021 Final Regular-Season Standings

AFC EAST	W-L-T	AFC SOUTH	W-L-T	AFC NORTH	W-L-T	AFC WEST	W-L-T
Bills	11–6	Titans	12–5	Bengals	10–7	Chiefs	12–5
Patriots	10–7	Colts	9–8	Steelers	9–7–1	Raiders	10–7
Dolphins	9–8	Texans	4–13	Browns	8–9	Chargers	9–8
Jets	4–13	Jaguars	3–14	Ravens	8–9	Broncos	7–10

NFC EAST	W-L-T	NFC SOUTH	W-L-T	NFC NORTH	W-L-T	NFC WEST	W-L-T
Cowboys	12–5	Buccaneers	13–4	Packers	13–4	Rams	12–5
Eagles	9–8	Saints	9–8	Vikings	8–9	Cardinals	11–6
Washington	7–10	Falcons	7–10	Bears	6–11	49ers	10–7
Giants	4–13	Panthers	5–12	Lions	3–13–1	Seahawks	7–10

Weeks 1-4

WEEK 1

✳ That Man Again:
The GOAT started where he left off, making opposing defenses look silly. Super Bowl champ **Tom Brady** and his Buccaneers beat the Cowboys 31-29 in a super-entertaining game that opened the 2021 season. Brady threw 4 TD passes, while **Dak Prescott** for Dallas was almost as good, throwing 3. It was a back-and-forth game, but Dallas left Tom Terrific too much time. He led the Bucs to a game-winning field goal by **Ryan Succop** in the final seconds.

✳ Saints Surprise: **Aaron Rodgers**
didn't look like an NFL MVP in the Green Bay Packers' first game. His opposing QB, **Jameis Winston** of the New Orleans Saints, looked like he would be an award-winner, throwing 5 TD passes as his team smacked the Pack 38-3.

✳ Extra Time:
The NFL started having overtime regular-season games in 1974. But the OT game between the Cincinnati Bengals and Minnesota Vikings was a first. Minnesota tied the game in regulation with a last-play field goal. Then the Bengals needed all 10 minutes of OT before they kicked their own last-play-of-OT field goal for the 27-24 win.

✳ So Close!:
The unlucky Cleveland Browns were very good, but just not good enough. They led the defending AFC-champion Kansas City Chiefs until the fourth quarter, but made one mistake too many. That let QB **Patrick Mahomes** back in the game, and he threw 2 late TDs to clinch a 33-29 comeback win.

WEEK 2

✳ Tale of Two Kickers:
Minnesota's **Greg Joseph** missed a last-play field goal that would have given the Vikings a win over the Cardinals. Instead, led by QB **Kyler Murray**'s 400 yards passing, Arizona won 34-33. Meanwhile, Dallas K **Greg Zuerlein** did come through for his team. His 56-yarder gave the Cowboys a 20-17 win over the Chargers.

✳ Titanic:
Tennessee came through in overtime to beat Seattle 33-30. RB **Derrick Henry** was

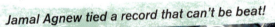
Jamal Agnew tied a record that can't be beat!

the star, powering for 182 yards and 2 late scores. After stopping the Seahawks in OT, the Titans drove for **Randy Bullock**'s 36-yard game-winning kick.

✴ Flip for Six: Baltimore QB **Lamar Jackson** did a huge flip as he scored the game-winning TD in the Ravens' 36-35 win over the Chiefs. It was his second score of the day, as the former NFL MVP beat Kansas City for the first time in his career.

WEEK 3

✴ What a Kick!:

Baltimore's **Justin Tucker** launched a 66-yard field goal—the longest in NFL history!—on the final play of the Ravens' game against Detroit. The ball flew and flew . . . bounced on the crossbar . . . and went over! Good! The Ravens won 19-17.

Justin Tucker

✴ Welcome to the NFL: Chicago first-round pick QB **Justin Fields** got his first NFL start against the Cleveland Browns. He probably wishes he had waited. Cleveland sacked Fields nine times (**Myles Garrett** had 4.5 of them to set a Browns record). Chicago had one yard passing and only 47 total yards in the 26-6 wipeout.

✴ Can't Be Topped: Arizona tried a wild play at the end of the first half of its game with Jacksonville: a 68-yard field-goal attempt. It was just short, and the Jaguars' **Jamal Agnew** caught the ball at the back of the end zone. Next stop: the other

end zone! After a 109-yard return, he had scored a shocking TD, tying the record for longest NFL play ever. It was not enough, however, and Arizona won 31-19.

WEEK 4

✴ New York, New York: Both teams from America's biggest city entered Week 4 winless. Then both put together overtime wins! The Titans came back to tie the Jets but **Matt Ammendola** kicked a game-winning field goal for a 27-24 Jets win. The Giants trailed the Saints by 11 points in the fourth quarter. However, QB **Daniel Jones** led the team to a 21-21 tie. In overtime, RB **Saquon Barkley** scored to give the Giants a 27-21 win.

✴ Homecoming:

Brady came back to play in New England for the first time since he left the Patriots. A rainy, windy night made the going tough for both teams. Still, Brady showed his former Patriots fans the old magic. He led the Bucs to a late field goal and a 19-17 win. In the game, Brady became the NFL's all-time leader in passing yards, too.

✴ Big Bad Bills: Buffalo moved to 3–1 by stomping the Texans 40-0. That gave the Bills two shutouts in a season for the first time since 1990. The defense had 4 interceptions and recovered a fumble, while **Tyler Bass** had 4 field goals for the Bills.

Weeks 5-8

WEEK 5

✱ Four Misses and a Make:

Green Bay K **Mason Crosby** is usually automatic. He was anything but against Cincinnati. He missed a field goal and an extra point, then missed another kick that would have won the game in the fourth quarter. And he missed his first kick in overtime! Finally, the Packers got him one more chance, and he made it to give Green Bay a 25-22 win.

✱ Undefeated: The Arizona Cardinals
were the only unbeaten team left after five weeks. Led by rising star **Kyler Murray**, the Cardinals beat the 49ers 17-10. A great late TD catch by **DeAndre Hopkins** sealed the win. It was the first time the Cards had started 5–0 since 1974.

✱ Tough Record: Jacksonville
lost 37-19 to Tennessee. It was the Jaguars' 20th loss in a row, including some from 2020. That gave them the second longest losing streak in NFL history! RB **Derrick Henry** scored three times and ran for 130 yards to lead the way for Tennessee.

WEEK 6

✱ Finally!: The Jaguars left the country
and came back winners. In a game played in London, England, Jacksonville beat Miami 23-20. **Matthew Wright** kicked a 53-yard field goal on the final play.

✱ Cowboy Up: The Cowboys beat the
Patriots in New England for the first time since 1987, and they needed overtime to do it. After tying the game on a **Greg Zuerlein** field goal, Dallas used a TD pass from **Dak Prescott** to **CeeDee Lamb** to win 35-29.

✱ Forcing a Win: Steelers LB **T.J.
Watt** forced Seattle QB **Geno Smith** to fumble late in overtime. That gave the Steelers a shot at a game-winning field goal and **Chris Boswell** didn't miss. Pittsburgh thrilled the hometown fans by snatching a 23-20 win.

WEEK 7

✱ New Stars: Cincinnati's **Joe
Burrow** and **Ja'Marr Chase** played together at LSU, and now they're both in

Jets QB Mike White

Fumble! Pittsburgh defensive star T.J. Watt forced Seattle's Geno Smith to cough up the ball!

the NFL. The teammates teamed up for an 82-yard TD on the way to a 41-17 win over Baltimore. Chase had 201 receiving yards to set a team rookie record (that he later broke in Week 17!). Burrow had 416 passing yards, most so far in his short career. A big win for a young team.

★ Mr. 600: **Tom Brady** became the first player in NFL history to reach 600 career TD passes. The 44-year-old had 4 scoring passes in Tampa Bay's 38-3 win over Chicago. The second was No. 600. **Mike Evans** caught it and gave the football to a fan in the stands by mistake! The fan gave it back so Brady could keep the souvenir.

★ NFL Scoring First: Arizona remained unbeaten with a 31-5 win over Houston. But the big news was that this was the first NFL game ever—since 1920!—to finish with that exact score!

WEEK 8
★ And Then There Were None:
The Packers knocked off the unbeaten Cardinals in an exciting Thursday-night game. The Green Bay defense didn't let

Kyler Murray have much room, but he still had a final chance to win the game. But the Packers' **Rasul Douglas** made an end-zone interception to seal his team's 24-21 win.

★ Cooper to Cooper: With star Dallas QB **Dak Prescott** out with an injury, Cooper Rush stepped up for the first start of his four-year NFL career. He led the Cowboys to a 20-16 win over Minnesota. Rush made the winning pass to **Amari Cooper** with less than a minute left.

★ The Jets . . . Won?: The Jets' tough season got a big highlight with an upset win over Cincinnati 34-31. QB **Mike White** made his first start and set an NFL record by completing 37 passes in his debut. He also threw 3 TD passes and even caught a two-point conversion pass.

★ Upset in New Orleans: The Saints lost starting QB **Jameis Winston** in the second quarter, but still found a way to upset the 6-1 Buccaneers with backup **Trevor Siemian** at the controls. The Saints picked off two passes, returning the second for a clinching TD in the 36-27 win.

Weeks 9–12

WEEK 9

★ Upset City: Big upsets are rare in the NFL, so to have three in one weekend was pretty wild. First, the 15-point underdog Jaguars shocked the Bills, beating them 9-6. A big reason was that Jacksonville's **Josh Allen** (a linebacker) took over the game from Buffalo's **Josh Allen** (a QB). LB Allen had a sack, an interception, and a fumble recovery, plus eight tackles. Meanwhile, Denver mostly shut down Dallas's NFL No. 1 offense in a surprising 30-16 win. Finally, the Titans manhandled the Rams in Los Angeles 28-16. A pick-six by **Kevin Byard** was a key early score for Tennessee, who won without injured NFL rushing leader **Derrick Henry**.

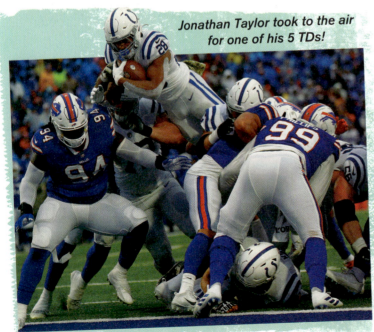

Jonathan Taylor took to the air for one of his 5 TDs!

WEEK 10

★ Superman Returns: Carolina let QB **Cam "Superman" Newton** go earlier in the year. Then their starter **Sam Darnold** was injured. Calling Superman! Newton returned and scored a rushing TD and threw a TD pass to lead the Panthers to a 34-10 upset of the 8–1 Cardinals.

★ He's Back!: After a bumpy start to the season (10 interceptions in nine games), Kansas City QB **Patrick Mahomes** showed why he was one of the league's best. Against the rival Raiders, he threw 5 TD passes. He even completed a pass left-handed! The Chiefs won 41-14 to stay on top of the AFC West.

★ Lions Don't Lose!: For the first time in 2021, the Detroit Lions didn't lose. Then again, they didn't win, either. Detroit tied Pittsburgh 16-16, the first NFL tie since early in 2020. Pittsburgh was without starting QB **Ben Roethlisberger**, out due to COVID rules. Neither team could score in the 10-minute OT period.

★ Tampa Surprise: Washington had one of the worst records in the NFC. Tampa Bay had one of the best. But that's why they play the games! Washington intercepted **Tom Brady**

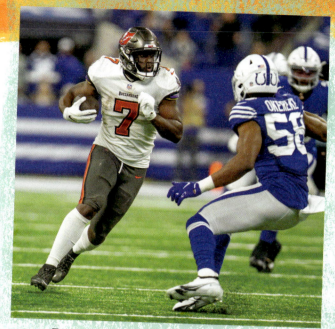

Fournette inspired the Bucs to a big win.

with the Bills' loss to Indy, and the Brady-less Patriots were back in first place in the AFC East.

WEEK 12

✱ Spoiled Turkey: Las Vegas ruined Dallas's feast, winning 36-33 in overtime on Thanksgiving Day. Dallas had to score twice in the last three minutes of the fourth quarter to tie the game, but then couldn't move the ball in overtime, setting up the Raiders' game-winning field goal. The teams combined for a surprising 28 penalties in the game.

✱ Four for Fournette: Tampa Bay RB **Leonard Fournette** ran for a 28-yard TD with less than 30 seconds left to nail down a 38-31 comeback win for the Bucs over the Colts. It was Fournette's fourth TD of the game. He also made a powerful halftime speech when his team trailed 24-14. Teammates said they were inspired to come out and play better—and they did!

✱ Sweep: Cincinnati beat Pittsburgh 41-10 to complete its first season sweep of the teams' two annual games since 2009. **Joe Mixon** ran for 165 yards, the most of his career, and scored twice. **Mike Hilton** had a big play, returning an interception 24 yards for a TD.

✱ Rams Turn to Lambs: The Rams lost their third straight game, 36-28 to the Packers. QB **Matthew Stafford** gave up a pick-six for the third straight game—not a good streak to own! Green Bay QB **Aaron Rodgers** was playing with a broken toe, but still managed to run for a score while also throwing 2 TD passes.

twice and beat the Super Bowl champs 29-19 in a big upset.

WEEK 11

✱ Touchdown Taylor: Colts RB **Jonathan Taylor** ran wild in a surprising 41-15 upset over the Bills in Buffalo. Taylor scored a career-high 5 TDs and ran for 185 yards.

✱ No Lamar? No Problem!: Baltimore star QB **Lamar Jackson** got sick right before his team's game with the Bears. **Tyler Huntley** stepped in at the last minute and brought home a 16-13 win. He led the Ravens on the 72-yard game-winning drive that finished with a TD run by **Devonta Freeman** with just 22 seconds left.

✱ Pats on D: New England won its fifth straight game, and the defense was a big reason. They shut out the Atlanta Falcons, capping a 25-0 win with a pick-six by **Kyle Van Noy** in the fourth quarter. Combined

Weeks 13-16

WEEK 13

★ Joy in Detroit:
The Lions won their first game in 364 days with a thrilling late drive. Trailing Minnesota 27-23, Detroit took over with less than two minutes left and no timeouts. QB **Jared Goff** made some great key throws. After an incompletion, they were left with four seconds to play and 11 yards to go. Goff zipped a TD pass to **Amon-Ra St. Brown** to set off a team celebration for the 29-27 win.

★ Bold Move:
Baltimore coach **John Harbaugh** called for a two-point try after his Ravens pulled to within a point on a late TD pass from **Lamar Jackson** to **Sammy Watkins**. But the attempt failed and Pittsburgh held on for a 20-19 win.

★ Touchdown Taylor:
The Colts romped over the Texans, led by star RB **Jonathan Taylor**. With 143 rushing yards, he took over the NFL lead in that stat. His 2 TDs added to his NFL lead of 16; that total also tied a new Colts' team record—the old record was set way back in 1964! Indy won 31-0.

WEEK 14

★ Big West Wins:
The NFC West race got tighter when the Rams beat the Cardinals in Arizona 30-23. The Rams were missing several players to injury and COVID but found a way to win. The big plays were 3 TD passes from **Matthew Stafford** and key interceptions by the Rams D. A day earlier, San Francisco beat Cincinnati 26-23 in overtime when **Brandon Aiyuk**

dove into the end zone on a 12-yard scoring play after the Bengals had taken the OT lead with a field goal.

★ Titan Power:
Tennessee got back on track with a 20-0 win over Jacksonville and moved 9–4, tied for best in the AFC. The Titans' defense picked off 4 Jags passes and sacked **Trevor Lawrence** 3 times. It was the first time Jacksonville had been shut out since 2009.

★ Sad Day:
Denver honored former receiver **Demaryius Thomas**, who died suddenly at home, with uniform patches and a moment of silence. Inspired, they then stomped the Lions 38-10. After several touchdowns, the players gathered near Thomas's No. 88, which had been painted on the field.

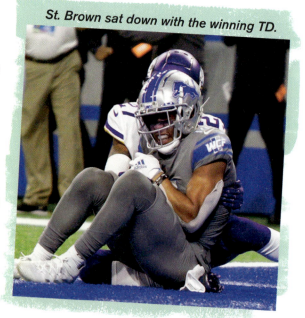

St. Brown sat down with the winning TD.

TE Mike Gesecki helped Miami leap over New Orleans.

WEEK 15

★ Pack Is Back: Green Bay clinched the NFC North division title and moved to the top of the NFC. **Aaron Rodgers** had 3 TDs, moving into a tie for the Packers' career record as the Pack beat Baltimore 31-30. For the second time, the Ravens went for two after a late score, but failed, leading to the loss.

★ Upset of the Year: Detroit had won only one game, while Arizona had the NFC's best record. But **Jared Goff** led the Lions to a shocking 30-12 win over the Cards. Detroit kept Arizona QB **Kyler Murray** from working his magic; Goff threw 3 TD passes.

★ A Surprise Shutout: For the first time since 2006, an offense led by **Tom Brady** was shut out. The Saints kept the Bucs from scoring and won 9-0. Tampa Bay lost three key players to injury, leaving Brady with few weapons to work with.

★ A Full Kupp: **Cooper Kupp** broke the Rams' record for catches in a season, including 2 for TDs, as the Rams held on to beat Seattle 20-10. The game was played on a Tuesday after COVID tests forced a move from Sunday's scheduled start.

WEEK 16

★ Chargers Shocked: The Texans had one of the NFL's worst records, while the Chargers were eyeing a playoff spot. But the records didn't matter as Houston pulled off a huge upset. It's true that the Chargers were missing some key players sick with COVID, but the Texans had 10 starters on the COVID list and still managed to force 3 turnovers. Houston's offense rolled, led by RB **Rex Burkhead**'s career-best 149 yards in the 41-29 win.

★ To the Top of the East: Buffalo knocked off New England to grab first place in the AFC East with just two games left to play. QB **Josh Allen** threw not 1 but 2 backhanded flip passes for touchdowns. **Micah Hyde** picked off 2 Patriots passes, too, in the 33-21 victory.

★ Cowboys Stampede: Dallas piled up its highest points total since 1980 while romping over Washington 56-14. **Dak Prescott** had 4 TD passes en route to a 42-7 halftime lead, while the Cowboys also scored on an interception return and a blocked punt! The Cowboys also clinched the NFC East championship.

★ Lucky 7: The Dolphins beat the Saints 20-3 and set a new NFL record. Miami became the first team ever with a seven-game losing streak and a seven-game winning streak in the same season. The win over the Saints moved the Dolphins to 8–7 with a shot at the playoffs. That chance seemed a long way off when they were 1–7 in November.

Weeks 17-18

Carlson capped off two big Vegas wins.

WEEK 17

★ Bengals Roar:
What a pair of weeks for QB **Joe Burrow** of the Bengals! First, he set a Cincinnati team record with 525 yards passing in Week 16. It was also the fourth-highest single-game total in NFL history. The Bengals beat the Ravens 41-21. Then in Week 17, he added 446 more yards. His 971-yard total was the most in back-to-back wins in NFL history! The win helped Cincy clinch its first AFC North title since the 2015 season.

★ One More to Go:
After Indianapolis tied the game 20-20, Las Vegas QB **Derek Carr** and WR **Hunter Renfrow** teamed up for a key 24-yard pass play as the Raiders drove down the field with less than two minutes to go. **Daniel Carlson** made a 33-yard field goal on the game's final play— Las Vegas 23, Indy 20.

WEEK 18

★ Colts Stumble:
If the Colts beat the 3–13 Jaguars, they were in the playoffs. Oops. **Carson Wentz** had the worst game of his career, the Jaguars played their best. Indy lost 26-11 in a Week 18 shocker.

★ Big Ben Comes Back:
Pittsburgh QB **Ben Roethlisberger** is on his way to the Hall of Fame. In his last regular-season game, he showed why. He gave the Steelers the lead against the Ravens late in the game with a TD pass to **Chase Claypool**. After Baltimore tied it to force overtime, Big Ben did it again. With less than two minutes left and a playoff spot on the line, he led the team to a game-winning field goal and a 16-13 win.

★ Crazy in Vegas:
The regular season ended on Sunday night with one final game, and it was one of the wildest of the season. The Raiders hosted the Chargers. The winner went to the playoffs. The loser went home. However, if the teams tied, both would earn playoff spots and the Steelers would be out. The Chargers fell behind early, but QB **Justin Herbert** steered them to a late-game tie at 29-29. In overtime, both teams kicked field goals, so it was still tied! Vegas moved the ball down the field with less than a minute to go. If they just knelt down, the game would end 32-32. The Raiders didn't settle. A last running play set up another game-winning Carlson field goal. Vegas got its first playoff spot since 2016. The Chargers went home, their season over.

Wild-Card Weekend

AFC
Bills 47, Patriots 17

Josh Allen led the way with 5 TD passes, 2 to TE Dawson Knox, as the Bills ran their winning streak to five games. Buffalo also gave Patriots' coach **Bill Belichick** the worst playoff loss of his career.

Bengals 26, Raiders 19

Cincinnati won its first playoff game since 1991. The win ended the longest run without a playoff victory in the NFL among current teams. **Joe Burrow**'s TD pass to **Tyler Boyd** was the key score. **Evan McPherson** also had 4 field goals.

Chiefs 42, Steelers 21

Patrick Mahomes matched Allen with 5 TD passes while also piling up 404 yards in the air. TE **Travis Kelce** became the first player ever with a TD catch, a TD pass, and 100-plus receiving yards in the same postseason game. The Steelers' loss was the last for star QB Roethlisberger, who said he was retiring after an 18-year career.

NFC
Buccaneers 31, Eagles 15

Philadelphia never really had a chance against the defending Super Bowl champs. **Tom Brady** led his team to a 31-0 lead before the Eagles added 2 late touchdowns. WR **Mike Evans** had 117 receiving yards and TD for Tampa Bay.

49ers 23, Cowboys 17

San Francisco held on in a tight game as the clock ran out on the Cowboys before they could try one final shot at the end zone. **Deebo Samuel** was the 49ers' Mr. Everything. He ran for 72 yards and a score and also caught 3 passes for 38 yards. Dallas didn't help itself by being called for a franchise playoff-record-tying 14 penalties.

Rams 34, Cardinals 11

Matthew Stafford had started 182 NFL games without a playoff win, the most ever by a QB. That ended with his team's big win over the Cardinals. Stafford threw 2 TD passes and ran for another. The LA defense swarmed over **Kyler Murray** and added a pick-six.

Samuel did it all in the Niners' playoff win.

2021 Playoffs

DIVISIONAL PLAYOFFS

AFC

Bengals 19, Titans 16

The Titans sacked QB **Joe Burrow** a record-tying 9 times. But the Bengals' rookie kept bouncing back up and led his team to its first road playoff victory ever! K **Evan McPherson** nailed a 52-yard field goal on the final play to seal the upset of the No. 1 seed.

AFC

Chiefs 42, Bills 36

Wow! Fans are still catching their breath months later after this instant classic. The Bills put together incredible comebacks twice in the last two minutes on TD passes from **Josh Allen** to **Gabriel Davis** (who set an all-time NFL playoff record with 4 TD catches). But **Patrick Mahomes** never gave up. With just 13 seconds left after the Bills' last TD, he moved his team into position for a game-tying field goal. In overtime, the Chiefs got the ball first and marched to victory on a Mahomes-to-**Travis Kelce** TD. KC heads to its fourth AFC Championship Game in a row.

NFC

49ers 13, Packers 10

Another No. 1 seed fell in the snow at Green Bay. The 49ers upset the Packers and star QB **Aaron Rodgers**. A late blocked punt was returned for a tying TD for San Francisco. Then a final drive led by QB **Jimmy Garoppolo** ended with **Robbie Gould**'s game-winning kick.

Kelce's clutch TD catch ended one of the NFL's best games of 2021.

NFC
Rams 30, Buccaneers 27

What looked like a Rams rout turned into another **Tom Brady** miracle . . . almost. Los Angeles led 27-3 before fumbles and Brady magic helped Tampa Bay tie the score at 27-27. But the Bucs left Rams QB **Matthew Stafford** and superstar WR **Cooper Kupp** too much time. They teamed on 64 yards of pass plays to set up yet another game-winning kick, this time by **Matt Gay**.

CONFERENCE CHAMPIONSHIPS

AFC
Bengals 27, Chiefs 24

Two seasons ago, the Bengals were 2–14. For the 2021 season, they are AFC champs! Cincinnati completed this amazing comeback with a huge upset of Kansas City in the Chiefs' home stadium. Cincinnati trailed 21-3 after Mahomes had 3 TD passes in the first half. Then the Bengals' defense shut the Chiefs down in the second half. Meanwhile, Burrow led the Bengals on a record-tying 18-point comeback, including a big two-point conversion. Cincy took the lead 24-21, but KC tied it as time ran out. In overtime, **Vonn Bell** picked off a Mahomes pass. Burrow moved his team into position for McPherson's game-winning kick! On to the Super Bowl!

Joe Burrow was king of the AFC!

NFC
Rams 20, 49ers 17

The Rams had lost six games in a row to the 49ers. This time, they finally won. LA trailed 17-7 but scored the last 13 points of the game. Kupp continued his amazing season with 142 receiving yards and 2 TDs. The second TD pulled the Rams to within 17-14. Then Stafford drove the Rams to a pair of field goals by Gay to take the lead. With less than two minutes left, Garoppolo tried to come back. The Rams defense swarmed over him. Star DE **Aaron Donald** grabbed the QB as Garoppolo flung the ball up. **Travin Howard** picked off the wild pass to clinch the big win. The Rams went on to host the Super Bowl at its own SoFi Stadium. It's the second season in a row–and ever–that a home team will in the big game!

2021 NFL Awards

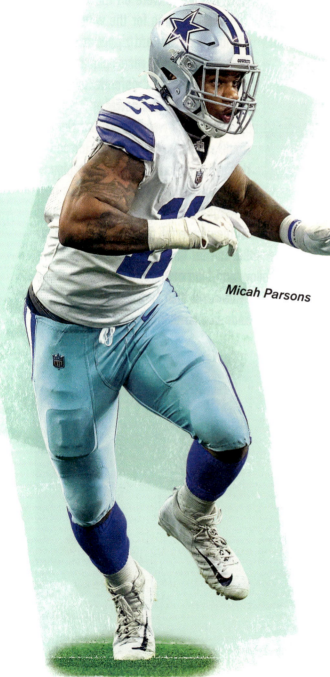

Micah Parsons

MOST VALUABLE PLAYER
AARON RODGERS
PACKERS

OFFENSIVE PLAYER OF THE YEAR
COOPER KUPP
RAMS

DEFENSIVE PLAYER OF THE YEAR
T.J. WATT
STEELERS

OFFENSIVE ROOKIE OF THE YEAR
JA'MARR CHASE
BENGALS

DEFENSIVE ROOKIE OF THE YEAR
MICAH PARSONS
COWBOYS

COACH OF THE YEAR
MIKE VRABEL
TITANS

WALTER PAYTON NFL MAN OF THE YEAR
ANDREW WHITWORTH
RAMS

2021 Stats Leaders

1,811 RUSHING YARDS
18 RUSHING TDS
Jonathan Taylor, Colts

5,316 PASSING YARDS
43 TD PASSES
Tom Brady, Buccaneers

145 RECEPTIONS
1,947 RECEIVING YARDS
16 RECEIVING TDS
Cooper Kupp, Rams

40 FIELD GOALS
Daniel Carlson, Raiders

11 INTERCEPTIONS
Trevon Diggs, Cowboys

192 TACKLES
Foyesade Oluokun, Falcons

150 POINTS
Daniel Carlson, Raiders; **Nick Folk**, Patriots

22.5 SACKS
T.J. Watt, Steelers

Jonathan Taylor

2022 Hall of Fame Class

Congrats to the newest members of the Pro Football Hall of Fame. Which of today's NFL players do you think will join them someday?

Three-time champ Cliff Branch

Tony Boselli T
Big and powerful three-time All-Pro, member of the 1990s All-Decade Team

Cliff Branch WR
Speedy pass-catcher who helped the Raiders win three Super Bowls

LeRoy Butler CB
A 1990s All-Decade player who helped the Packers reach two Super Bowls

Art McNally
A longtime NFL official who helped develop the instant-replay system

Sam Mills LB
Hard-hitting linebacker for the Saints and the Panthers and a key leader for both

Richard Seymour DE
Strong pass-rusher who won three Super Bowls with the Patriots

Dick Vermeil
A longtime NFL coach, he led the Eagles to an NFL title and the Rams to a Super Bowl win

Bryant Young DT
Another 1990s All-Decade star, he was a two-time All-Pro for the 49ers

2021 FANTASY STARS

Fantasy football fans had an extra game to play this season, too. As you look at your team for the 2022 season, remember that the per-game averages will be up a bit. If you compare 2021 to earlier seasons, the numbers will be a little higher!

POSITION/PLAYER/POINTS*

QB **Josh Allen** 402.58

RB **Jonathan Taylor** 343.80

WR **Cooper Kupp** 439.50

TE **Mark Andrews** 301.10

K **Daniel Carlson** 162.00

DEF **Cowboys** 177.00

*Per NFL.com

New Faces → New Places!

NFL fans were probably dizzy after one of the busiest offseasons in years. Not long after the Rams Super Bowl victory parade, big-name players started changing teams. Some were trades, others were free-agent signings. But in either case, there were some very surprising moves (Russell Wilson?!) and some that were expected. But here's a quick guide to the biggest and most important moves for the 2022 season.

PLAYER/POS	OLD TEAM	NEW TEAM
Tom Brady, QB	Bucs	Bucs*
Russell Wilson, QB	Seahawks	Broncos
Davante Adams, WR	Packers	Raiders
Matt Ryan, QB	Falcons	Colts
Carson Wentz, QB	Colts	Commanders
Deshaun Watson, QB	Texans	Browns
Mitchel Trubisky, QB	Bears	Steelers
Tyreek Hill, WR	Chiefs	Dolphins
Von Miller, LB	Rams	Bills
Allen Robinson, WR	Bears	Rams
Khalil Mack, LB	Bears	Chargers
J.C. Jackson, CB	Patriots	Chargers

*You probably heard this already, but **Tom Brady** retired for about a month before changing his mind! Tampa Bay fans were thrilled!

PICK SIX PICKS A NEW CHAMP!
The 2021 college football season saw a lot of great new talent and teams . . . and a new champion. For the first time since 1980, the Georgia Bulldogs wound up on top. They beat rival Alabama in the final, a 33-18 victory capped off by this Kelee Ringo (5) interception-return score.

COLLEGE FOOTBALL

College Football 2021

College football is getting more like college basketball every year. In hoops, it's all about the Final Four. Since the start of the College Football Playoff in 2014, the "final four" in football has become all-important. It seems like the Playoff starts almost from the first week of the fall season. Almost any loss by a highly ranked team can mean the end of its hopes to make that four.

In recent seasons, a handful of teams have dominated those all-important places. Alabama has been in all but one edition of the Playoff so far. Clemson has been in six, while Oklahoma

and Ohio State have been in four each. All of those teams were expected to compete once again for those final spots in 2021, but for the first time in a while, some surprises squeaked in. Clemson had a tough season and was out of it early. Oklahoma hung tough, but a late loss to Oklahoma State knocked them out.

Meanwhile, a pair of teams were climbing the rankings week by week. One was familiar: Michigan. While the Wolverines have struggled in recent seasons, they have a long history of greatness. When they beat rival Ohio State in November, they capped one of their best seasons in a long time. They earned one of the final spots. Meanwhile, a team from outside the Power 5 conferences (which are the SEC, ACC, Big 12, Big Ten, and Pac-12) finally made the final four. Cincinnati was really good in 2020 but was shut out of the final. When Oklahoma lost and the Bearcats remained undefeated, the selection committee had no choice. Welcome to the Playoff, Cincy!

Of course, there were lots more ups and downs to the season than just the Playoff teams, including a lot of COVID issues. Follow the whole season month by month starting on page 76.

While most of the attention was focused on

Cincinnati QB Desmond Ridder

TOP AWARDS

HEISMAN TROPHY (BEST PLAYER)
DAVEY O'BRIEN TROPHY (TOP QB)
Bryce Young/ALABAMA

WALTER CAMP AWARD (BEST PLAYER)
DOAK WALKER AWARD (BEST RB)
Kenneth Walker III/MICHIGAN

BRONKO NAGURSKI AWARD (TOP DEFENDER)
Will Anderson/ALABAMA

HOME DEPOT AWARD (TOP COACH)
Luke Fickell/CINCINNATI

Bryce Young accepts the Heisman Trophy.

the College Football Playoff teams and conferences, hundreds of other schools competed in the Football Championship Series (FCS). Most are smaller schools, but many have great football programs. In fact, FCS schools won 12 games over FBS teams in 2021; that's the most since 2000. Highlights of those inter-division upsets included Pac-12 schools Washington and Arizona losing to Montana and Northern Arizona. Jacksonville State shocked in-state rival Florida State. And UC Davis stunned Tulsa. So there's some pretty good football at these "lower" divisions.

Also, let's celebrate the champs from those FCS divisions:

FCS SUBDIVISION: North Dakota State
DIVISION II: Ferris State
DIVISION III: Mary Hardin-Baylor
NAIA: Morningside

Big schools or small schools, college football continues to thrill fans of all ages all over the country. How did your favorite team do this year? Read on to relive some of the biggest games of the year and then enjoy the excitement of the College Football Playoff!

FINAL TOP 10

1. **Georgia**
2. **Alabama**
3. **Michigan**
4. **Cincinnati**
5. **Baylor**
6. **Ohio State**
7. **Oklahoma State**
8. **Notre Dame**
9. **Michigan State**
10. **Oklahoma**

September

USC's
Jaxson Dart

➜ Big Bulldog Win: In a rare first-week matchup between top-five teams, No. 5 Georgia handed No. 3 Clemson a rare loss. The big play was an interception-return TD by Georgia's **Christopher Smith**. In a game dominated by defense, that was the only TD in the Bulldogs' big 10-3 win.

➜ Underdogs!: The Pac-12 got a shock when FCS school Montana knocked off No. 20 Washington 13-7.

➜ Busy Day: Speaking of the FCS, **Ren Hefley** of Presbyterian set a record with 10 TD passes as his team beat St. Andrews 84-43.

➜ Ducks Quack!: Oregon had never beaten Ohio State . . . and they first played each other back in 1958! That changed when the No. 12 Ducks ran right over the No. 3 Buckeyes 35-23. Oregon's **CJ Verdell** had 161 yards rushing and scored three times. It was Ohio State's first regular-season loss since 2018!

➜ Irish Escape: After needing overtime to beat Florida State in its first game, No. 8 Notre Dame faced another big challenge. The Fighting Irish scored a touchdown with just over a minute left to beat unranked Toledo 32-29.

➜ LA Shockers: Two Pac-12 teams based in Los Angeles were upset in September. First, No. 14 USC was blown out by unranked Stanford 42-28. The

Cardinal scored on an 87-yard run early and never looked back. Then No. 13 UCLA lost a heartbreaker to Fresno State 40-37. The Bruins took a lead with only 54 seconds left, but that left enough time for the Bulldogs to drive 75 yards for the winning TD.

➜ **Close Call:** Alabama's No. 1 ranking looked shaky after they barely beat No. 11 Florida. If not for a mistake on a two-point attempt late in the game, the Gators might have sent the game into overtime. Instead, 3 TD passes by Bama QB **Bryce Young** were enough in the 31-29 win.

➜ **Fabulous Freshman:** After losing to Stanford, USC was in shock. Against Washington State, they were in trouble. Starting QB **Kedon Slovis** was hurt. In stepped freshman **Jaxson Dart**. He became an instant star, throwing for 391 yards and 4 TDs in his first college game. The Trojans won 45-14.

➜ **Clemson Goes Down:** For the first time in 97 weeks, Clemson left the Top 10. The reason was a shocking upset win by North Carolina State. The Wolfpack needed two overtimes, but they got the winning TD pass from **Devin Leary** to set off a field-storming celebration after the 27-21 win.

➜ **Bowling Them Over:** Bowling Green was a 30-point underdog to the Minnesota Golden Gophers. No problem! The Falcons picked off two passes and shut down Minnesota's offense. Instead of losing by 30, Bowling Green won by four points, 14-10.

➜ **Rah, Rah, Razorbacks:** Arkansas leaped into the national-title picture with a big 20-10 upset win over No. 7 Texas A&M. Star QB **KJ Jefferson** threw 2 TD passes before he was knocked out with a knee injury. Unfortunately, Arkansas ran into the No. 2 Georgia Bulldogs a week later and lost 37-0!

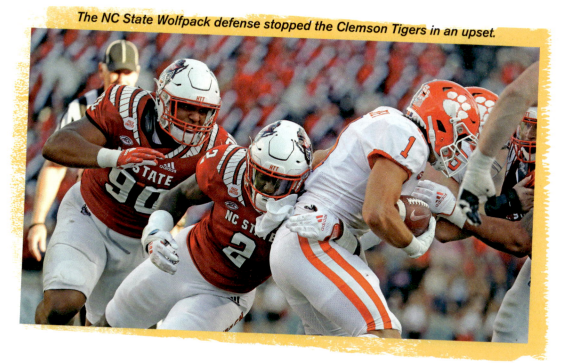

The NC State Wolfpack defense stopped the Clemson Tigers in an upset.

October

➜ **Super Cincy:** The No. 9 Bearcats took on No. 7 Notre Dame in a big showdown. It was the first time Cincinnati was in a battle of Top 10 teams. And they won! **Desmond Ridder** threw 2 TD passes for Cincy and ran for a score in the huge 24-13 win.

➜ **Oregon Oops:** The Ducks' chances for a perfect season ended with a shocking loss to Stanford. Oregon had stopped the Cardinal on the game's final play. But the Ducks committed a penalty, giving Stanford one more chance. **Tanner McKee** threw a TD pass that tied the game, and the Cardinal won in overtime 31-24.

➜ **Gator Bait:** Kentucky upset No. 10 Florida 20-13. The big play was a 76-yard TD return of a blocked field goal by Kentucky's **Trevin Wallace**. It was the first time since 1986 that the Wildcats had won a game on the Gators' home field.

➜ **Down Goes Bama!:** The biggest upset of recent seasons came on October 9 when unranked Texas A&M shocked No. 1 Alabama 41-38. It snapped Alabama's 100-game winning streak against unranked foes, ended the Crimson Tide's 19-game winning streak, and marked the first time **Nick Saban** had lost to one of his former assistant coaches (he had been 24–0). **Jimbo Fisher**'s A&M team tied the score at 38-38 on a TD pass from **Zach Calzada** to **Ainias Smith**. Then **Seth Small** hit a 28-yard field goal on the game's final play to win it.

➜ **Top Five Battle:** No. 3 Iowa came back from 14 points down to beat No. 4 Penn State 23-20. Fans stormed the field afterward to celebrate. Iowa remained unbeaten with a good shot at its first College Football Playoff spot.

➜ **Red River Classic:** The annual battle between Texas and Oklahoma is called the Red River Rivalry. It's named for the waterway that divides the two states. This season, No. 6 OU won 55-48 in a wild shootout that set a record for total points in the series' 117-game history. The Sooners were down 28-7 before tying the game. The teams then traded TDs until **Kennedy Brooks** ran 33 yards for the winning score with just seconds left in the game.

➜ **No More No. 2:** The Iowa Hawkeyes were thrilled to

Where did the field go? Hawkeyes fans celebrate a big win.

Kenneth Walker III dives for one of the five TDs he scored in Michigan State's big victory.

jump to No. 2 in the country after other top teams were upset. Then they were upset themselves by a surprisingly tough Purdue team. The Boilermakers held Iowa to just a single touchdown, while scoring in every quarter in the 24-7 win. The loss was even tougher for the Hawkeyes because it was played on Iowa's home field!

➜ Someone Has to Win: A new college football rule began in 2021. In overtime, teams try to score TDs or field goals first. If they can't or they are still tied after two overtimes, they take turns trying two-point conversions. Sort of like a penalty-kick shootout in soccer! Illinois upset No. 7 Penn State 20-18, and the rule got a big test. It took the teams *nine* overtimes to finish, the most ever in a college football game.

➜ Game of the Year?: For the first time in 123 years, Michigan and Michigan State faced off at 7–0 each. For the first time since 1964, both teams were in the top 10. It was one of the biggest games of the year and it played like one. State came back from 16 points down to win 37-33. **Kenneth Walker III** had 5 TDs for MSU. **Charles Brantley** picked off a Michigan pass with just over a minute left to seal the huge win.

➜ Return to Victory: SMU thought it was headed to overtime against Houston after they tied the score 37-37 with 30 seconds left. But the kickoff remained and Houston's **Marcus Jones** returned it 100 yards for a shocking TD that gave his team the win.

➜ Cougars Roar: The BYU Cougars kept the scoreboard operator busy in the game against Virginia. The two teams combined for 80 points (42-38 BYU) . . . in the first half alone! BYU's defense allowed just one Virginia touchdown in the second half, while its offense kept roaring to make the final score 66-49.

November

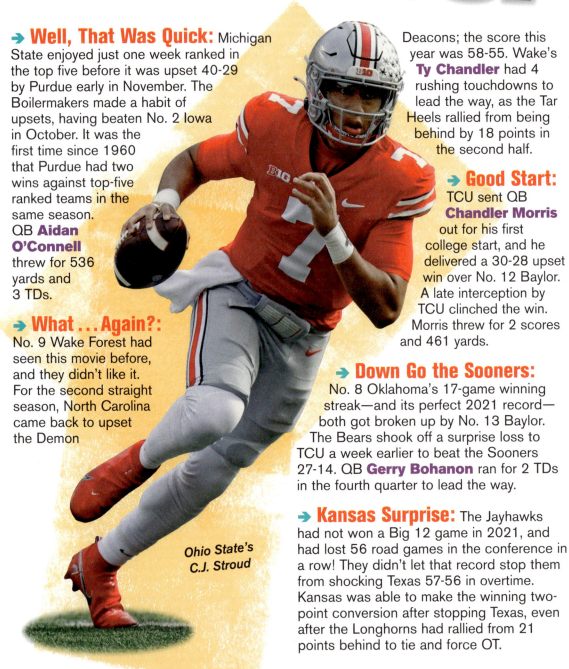

→ Well, That Was Quick: Michigan State enjoyed just one week ranked in the top five before it was upset 40-29 by Purdue early in November. The Boilermakers made a habit of upsets, having beaten No. 2 Iowa in October. It was the first time since 1960 that Purdue had two wins against top-five ranked teams in the same season. QB **Aidan O'Connell** threw for 536 yards and 3 TDs.

→ What . . . Again?: No. 9 Wake Forest had seen this movie before, and they didn't like it. For the second straight season, North Carolina came back to upset the Demon Deacons; the score this year was 58-55. Wake's **Ty Chandler** had 4 rushing touchdowns to lead the way, as the Tar Heels rallied from being behind by 18 points in the second half.

→ Good Start: TCU sent QB **Chandler Morris** out for his first college start, and he delivered a 30-28 upset win over No. 12 Baylor. A late interception by TCU clinched the win. Morris threw for 2 scores and 461 yards.

→ Down Go the Sooners: No. 8 Oklahoma's 17-game winning streak—and its perfect 2021 record— both got broken up by No. 13 Baylor. The Bears shook off a surprise loss to TCU a week earlier to beat the Sooners 27-14. QB **Gerry Bohanon** ran for 2 TDs in the fourth quarter to lead the way.

→ Kansas Surprise: The Jayhawks had not won a Big 12 game in 2021, and had lost 56 road games in the conference in a row! They didn't let that record stop them from shocking Texas 57-56 in overtime. Kansas was able to make the winning two-point conversion after stopping Texas, even after the Longhorns had rallied from 21 points behind to tie and force OT.

Ohio State's C.J. Stroud

➤ Answered Prayer: A long, last-second pass to the end zone is called a Hail Mary, after a famous prayer. South Dakota's prayers were answered when Carson Camp's Hail Mary heave was caught by **Jeremiah Webb** after being tipped by several players. Webb fell into the end zone as time ran out and South Dakota beat its in-state rival South Dakota State 23-20.

➤ Down Go the Ducks: Oregon had moved to No. 3 in the country, in a good spot to make the Playoff. Then they traveled to Utah and got smacked down. The Utes pounded the Ducks 38-7. A big play was a punt-return TD on the final play of the first half by **Britain Covey**.

➤ Rivalry Rout: UCLA and USC have played each other since 1929. In all that time, neither team had scored more than UCLA did in routing USC on November 20. The Bruins rolled to a 62-33 win. QB **Dorian Thompson-Robinson** threw 4 TD passes and ran for 2 scores. After one of them, he stopped to autograph a hat for a young fan—who was wearing USC colors!

➤ What a Half!: **C.J. Stroud** had a career game . . . in 30 minutes! The Ohio State QB threw for 6 TDs in the first half on the way to the No. 4 Buckeyes' 56-7 rout of No. 7 Michigan State. Stroud had only 3 incompletions and took most of the second half off!

➤ Wolverines Howl: Well, those woodland animals actually just sort of screech, but the No. 5 Michigan Wolverines did make a big noise. They beat No. 2 Ohio State 42-27, with **Hassan Haskins** running for 5 TDs. It was only the second time in 17 tries that Michigan has won the big rivalry game. The Wolverines got one more chance to howl, earning a spot in their first Big Ten Championship Game.

➤ Whew!: That's what Alabama fans were saying when their team survived with a 24-22 four-overtime win over rival Auburn. The Crimson Tide had to drive 97 yards to the tying touchdown late in the game. In overtime, the teams traded scores until Auburn could not complete a two-point conversion. The squeaker sent Alabama to yet another SEC title game against No. 1 Georgia.

Got a pen? Thompson-Robinson scored . . . and signed!

Conference Championships

SEC
ALABAMA 41
GEORGIA 24

The Crimson Tide handed the Bulldogs their first loss of the season. Alabama QB **Bryce Young** threw 3 TD passes and ran for another; his 421 passing yards were an SEC Championship Game record. Both teams, however, made it into the College Football Playoff.

BIG TEN
MICHIGAN 42
IOWA 3

The Wolverines punched their ticket to the Playoff with a rout of the Hawkeyes. **Blake Corum** ran for a 67-yard score, while RB **Donovan Edwards** threw a 75-yard TD pass to **Roman Wilson**. **Hassan Haskins** also ran for 2 scores. It was the Wolverines' first Big Ten title since 2004.

BIG 12
BAYLOR 21
OKLAHOMA STATE 16

Maybe an inch. That's how close Oklahoma State came to winning this game on the last play. **Dezmon Jackson** made a brave leap toward the corner of the end zone, but was pushed away at the last inch by Baylor's **Jairon McVea**. Baylor's upset win over the No. 5 team included another goal-line stand earlier in the game. OSU lost its chance for the Playoff.

PAC-12
UTAH 38
OREGON 10

No. 10 Oregon had lost its chance for the Playoff after losing to Stanford in October. Then it lost the Pac-12 title game to a strong Utah team. The Utes won their sixth straight game; a 23-0 halftime lead played a big part. The school then went on to its first-ever Rose Bowl.

Utah beat Oregon again in the Pac-12.

ACC
PITTSBURGH 45
WAKE FOREST 21

When your defense picks off 4 passes, you know you'll have a good day. When your QB (**Kenny Pickett**) also throws for 2 TDs and runs for another, that's icing on the cake. Pitt surprised the favored Demon Deacons for their first ACC title.

Bowl Games

Although COVID canceled some bowls, most of the games were played and several of them created memorable moments for fans and players.

ROSE BOWL
Ohio State 48, Utah 45

The Rose Bowl added another great game to its 108-year history. The Pac-12's Utah led most of the way, including 28-14 after a kickoff-return touchdown, but Ohio State battled back. QB **C.J. Stroud** set Rose Bowl records with 573 passing yards and 6 TD passes. Three of them went to **Jaxon Smith-Njigba**, who set an all-time all-bowl record with 347 receiving yards. Their last connection put OSU ahead 45-38. Utah then tied the game thanks to backup QB **Bryson Barnes**. But Stroud drove the Buckeyes to a game-winning 19-yard field goal by **Noah Ruggles**. What a game!

ALAMO BOWL
Oklahoma 47, Oregon 32

Both of these schools had their eye on the College Football Playoff. Both lost big games to miss that chance. So this bowl game was sort of like a consolation prize. Former longtime Oklahoma coach **Bob Stoops** led the Sooners after coach Lincoln Riley left to take over at USC. Stoops relied on RB **Kennedy Brooks**, who scored three times and ran for 142 yards.

DUKE'S MAYO BOWL
South Carolina 38, North Carolina 21

It was a Carolina battle, with SC storming out to an 18-0 lead and NC unable to catch up. SC's **Jaheim Bell** had 69- and 66-yard TD plays to lead the way. The best part of the bowl, though, was watching players dump a vat of mayonnaise on the head of SC coach **Shane Beamer**!

FIRST RESPONDER BOWL
Air Force 31, Louisville 28

Louisville came into this game with a history of great quarterback play (including former NFL MVP **Lamar Jackson** of the Baltimore Ravens). Although many of the Air Force students fly airplanes, its team usually depends on a great running attack. This game saw a big switch when Air Force QB **Haaziq Daniels** led the way with 2 TD passes and 252 passing yards.

Yes, that is real mayo on Coach Beamer.

College Football Playoff

SEMIFINAL NO. 1
COTTON BOWL
Alabama 27, Cincinnati 6

This season, Cincinnati sounded a lot like Cinderella, but the Bearcats' magical ride ended with a loss to mighty Alabama. Cincinnati was the first team outside the Power Five conferences to earn a spot in the Playoff. But the Crimson Tide rolled over them, powered by RB **Brian Robinson Jr.**'s Alabama bowl-game record 204 rushing yards. Heisman Trophy–winning QB **Bryce Young** had a quiet game watching Robinson score. But he did connect with **Ja'Corey Brooks** on a big 44-yard TD pass late in the second quarter. Alabama has made all but one of the eight College Football Playoff tournaments.

Robinson rumbled!

Burton busted out!

SEMIFINAL NO. 2
ORANGE BOWL
Georgia 34, Michigan 11

Like Cincinnati, Michigan surprised many by making the Playoff. They were the first team to start outside the Top 25 rankings to rise to the semifinal. Georgia came in a bit mad after losing its first game of the year to Alabama a few weeks earlier. QB **Stetson Bennett** had his way with the Michigan defense, throwing 3 TD passes. Georgia scored the first five times it had the ball, too. A 57-yard TD pass to **Jermaine Burton** capped the streak and gave Georgia a 27-3 halftime lead.

National Championship Game

Georgia 33, Alabama 18

Every time Georgia had come close to winning a title, it seemed like Alabama was in the way. Alabama won when the teams met in the 2017 national championship game . . . the 2018 SEC championship game and . . . even the 2021 SEC championship game, which was played only 37 days before this contest. Could the Bulldogs finally beat the Crimson Tide when it counted most?

The answer came in a 2021 College Football Championship that went down to the wire. Alabama led 9-6 at halftime. Georgia led 13-9 after the third quarter. Then came a crazy fourth quarter, when 29 of the game's 51 points were scored.

Alabama took the lead after Georgia quarterback **Stetson Bennett** fumbled. But Bennett, who started as a walk-on, put the Bulldogs ahead with a long touchdown pass to **Adonai Mitchell**. He threw another touchdown pass with only three minutes left. Georgia was now ahead by eight points, but Alabama could still force overtime with a touchdown and two-point conversion.

As the Tide rolled down the field, there came a play that no Georgia Bulldogs fan will ever forget. Defensive back **Kelee Ringo**

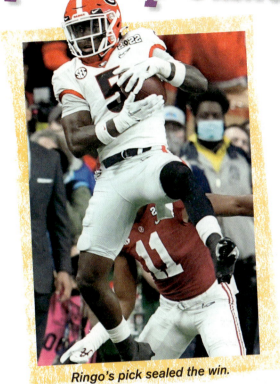

Ringo's pick sealed the win.

intercepted a pass with only 30 seconds left—and returned it 79 yards for a touchdown!

When Georgia coach **Kirby Smart** saw Ringo running toward the end zone, he was filled with joy. He knew his Bulldogs were about to be champions. "When that ball was in the air I said, 'he's going to catch this thing and we're going to win this game.' And he did."

It was Georgia's first national championship since 1980, and the first time it had beaten Alabama in any game since 2007. They picked a good time to break that streak!

WNBA/NBA

Hotels.com

BACK ON TOP!
The Golden State Warriors had the NBA's worst record two seasons ago, thanks to injuries and poor play. But in 2022, they returned to the top of the league for the fourth time in eight seasons, knocking off the Boston Celtics. Star guard Stephen Curry was the Finals MVP for his amazing shooting and fiery leadership. Read about the 2021 WNBA and the 2021–22 NBA inside!

WNBA 2021

*WNBA MVP
Jonquel Jones*

The Connecticut Sun put together one of the best WNBA seasons in recent years, ending the season with a 14-game winning streak. Their 26–6 regular-season mark was the best in team history, too. Leading the way were **Jonquel Jones**, **Brionna Jones**, and **DeWanna Bonner**. The Sun surprised many preseason experts by earning the top seed.

The Las Vegas Aces were not a big surprise. Led by 2020 MVP **A'ja Wilson** and with returning scoring star **Kelsey Plum**, the Aces won 24 games, following a 2020 season when they won 18 games (tied for the league lead) and reached the WBNA Finals. Together, those two teams earned byes into the WNBA semifinals, while teams ranked third through eighth had to battle for the chance to play the top two.

All those teams took a month off in the middle of the season to let the top players take part in the 2021 Summer Olympics. A total of 29 current players played the five-a-side or 3x3 events. Also, 22 former WNBA players joined teams including Australia, Canada, and Spain, all fought for gold. Did all that extra action slow down some WNBA teams? Seattle

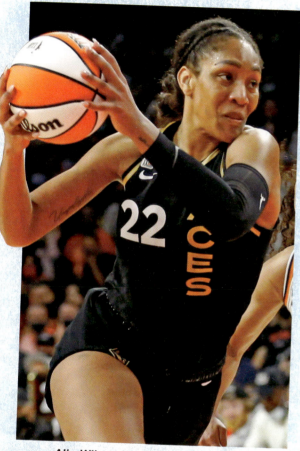

A'ja Wilson helped the Aces thrive.

Stat Leaders

23.4 Points
Tina Charles, Washington

11.9 Rebounds
Jonquel Jones, Connecticut

8.6 Assists
Courtney Vandersloot, Chicago

1.8 Steals
Brittney Sykes, Las Vegas

Award Winners

MOST VALUABLE PLAYER
Jonquel Jones, Connecticut

ROOKIE OF THE YEAR
Michaela Onyenwere, New York

DEFENSIVE PLAYER OF THE YEAR
Sylvia Fowles, Minnesota

SIXTH PLAYER OF THE YEAR
Kelsey Plum, Las Vegas

MOST IMPROVED PLAYER
Brionna Jones, Connecticut

COACH OF THE YEAR
Curt Miller, Connecticut

might have lost a bit of a spark with so many players making the trip to Tokyo, but they still made the playoffs.

But the league roared back into action after the Olympic break. While the Sun and Aces flew ahead of the pack, the other playoff teams were looking to break through for an upset win. After several exciting rounds of the playoffs, one of those surprise teams did come out on top. To find out who, read on!

WNBA Playoffs

Taurasi shot the Mercury to the Finals.

Round 1

Chicago 81, Dallas 64

Kahleah Copper led the way with 23 points for the Sky.

Phoenix 83, New York 82

A last-second free throw by **Brianna Turner** was the difference in this tight game.

Round 2

Chicago 89, Minnesota 76

The Sky made it two in a row with an upset of the No. 3–seed Lynx. **Courtney Vandersloot** scored 19 to lead Chicago.

Phoenix 85, Seattle 80 (OT)

WNBA legend **Sue Bird** lost to another legend, **Diana Taurasi** of Phoenix. The Suns' **Brittney Griner** was the big star, though, scoring 23 points and nabbing 16 rebounds.

Semifinals

Chicago 3, Connecticut 1

For only the third time in WNBA history, a team without a winning regular-season record will be in the Finals. Chicago, who finished 16–16, shocked No. 1–seeded Connecticut, led by former Sparks star **Candace Parker**. She scored 17 points in the clincher.

Phoenix 3, Las Vegas 2

They don't call Taurasi the GOAT for nothing. The WNBA's all-time scoring leader poured in 24 points, including 14 in the final quarter, as the Mercury earned a trip to the WNBA Finals. Griner scored 28 to show she's pretty great herself!

WNBA Finals

GAME 1 **Chicago** **91**
Phoenix **77**

Chicago did not care that they had a losing record in the regular season. This is the Finals, and the only thing that counts is the scoreboard. The Sky used a 21-2 run to nail down the victory. **Kahleah Copper** led the way with 21 points.

GAME 2 **Phoenix** **91**
Chicago **86** (OT)

Diana Taurasi led the with eight big points in overtime as Phoenix evened the series. **Brittney Griner** had a game-high 29 points. She also thrilled fans with her first dunk in the WNBA playoffs.

GAME 3 **Chicago** **86**
Phoenix **50**

This was a surprising rout of a star-studded team. Copper led the way with 22 points, 20 of which came in the first half. After speeding to a big lead, Chicago poured it on. The victory margin of 36 points was the largest in WNBA Finals history.

GAME 4 **Chicago** **80**
Phoenix **74**

Down by seven points with less than five minutes to play, Chicago saw its chance at

Parker brought a title to Chicago.

winning the title on its home court slipping away. But a late charge put them back in front to stay. In her hometown, former LA Sparks star **Candace Parker** held up the Sky's first WNBA championship trophy. **Allie Quigley** led the way with 26 points, while star guard **Courtney Vandersloot** had 15 assists. The Sky became the lowest-seeded team to win the WNBA title.

2021-22 NBA

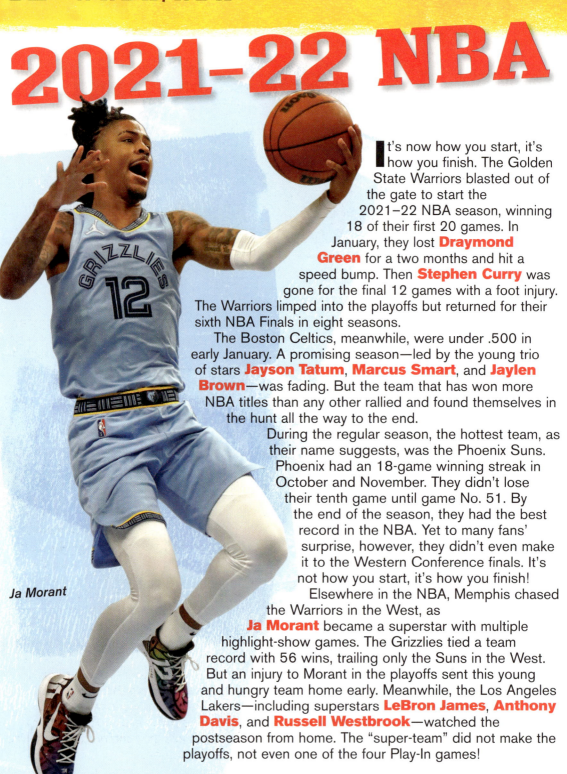

Ja Morant

It's now how you start, it's how you finish. The Golden State Warriors blasted out of the gate to start the 2021–22 NBA season, winning 18 of their first 20 games. In January, they lost **Draymond Green** for a two months and hit a speed bump. Then **Stephen Curry** was gone for the final 12 games with a foot injury. The Warriors limped into the playoffs but returned for their sixth NBA Finals in eight seasons.

The Boston Celtics, meanwhile, were under .500 in early January. A promising season—led by the young trio of stars **Jayson Tatum**, **Marcus Smart**, and **Jaylen Brown**—was fading. But the team that has won more NBA titles than any other rallied and found themselves in the hunt all the way to the end.

During the regular season, the hottest team, as their name suggests, was the Phoenix Suns. Phoenix had an 18-game winning streak in October and November. They didn't lose their tenth game until game No. 51. By the end of the season, they had the best record in the NBA. Yet to many fans' surprise, however, they didn't even make it to the Western Conference finals. It's not how you start, it's how you finish!

Elsewhere in the NBA, Memphis chased the Warriors in the West, as **Ja Morant** became a superstar with multiple highlight-show games. The Grizzlies tied a team record with 56 wins, trailing only the Suns in the West. But an injury to Morant in the playoffs sent this young and hungry team home early. Meanwhile, the Los Angeles Lakers—including superstars **LeBron James**, **Anthony Davis**, and **Russell Westbrook**—watched the postseason from home. The "super-team" did not make the playoffs, not even one of the four Play-In games!

Scoring champ Joel Embiid . . . from Cameroon!

What brings me the most joy . . . is seeing the guys who won it the first time. You always want that first-time feeling back. You never get it again, and the only way I can is to feel it through [our young players]. — DRAYMOND GREEN OF THE CHAMPION WARRIORS

One reason Brooklyn struggled was because point guard **Kyrie Irving** refused to get a COVID shot. That meant he could not play home games for the team, due to New York City rules, until late March.

The Sixers were part of a tight group of top teams in the Eastern Conference. With just six games left in the season, four teams had a chance at the best record in the conference. Miami, Boston, and Milwaukee joined Philly—all were aiming to end up No. 1. It was not decided until the final day, when Miami clinched the top spot. The Sixers not only made the playoffs, but they also had the top scorer. **Joel Embiid**, who was born in Cameroon, became the first center since 2000 and first international player to lead the NBA in scoring. And the Celtics were three games under .500 in January, but roared back to earn the No. 2 seed.

The NBA playoffs were packed with excitement, too. How exciting? Neither of the top teams in either conference made the NBA Finals! Read on!

In the Eastern Conference, one of the league's surprise teams was the Chicago Bulls. They had a nine-game winning streak to push their record to 27–11. **Lonzo Ball** emerged as a young star, along with veteran **Zach LaVine**. But they went 7–15 to end the season and were swept in the playoffs.

The East was the home of the NBA's biggest player move of the regular season. In January, Brooklyn traded **James Harden** to Philadelphia for star forward **Ben Simmons**. The move helped the Sixers, as the Nets faded (and because Simmons was injured and barely played).

In the Paint: 2021-22

Record Win: NBA teams are usually evenly matched. But some nights, one team is simply better—way better. In a December game, Memphis beat Oklahoma City 152-79. Do the math and you'll find the biggest victory margin in NBA history. It was also a single-game Grizzlies record for most points.

At the Buzzer: At the end of the Pelicans-Thunder game, the Pelicans' **Devonté Graham** figured, *why not*? As time ran out, he heaved up a shot from way past midcourt . . .and it went in! Game over, Pelicans win 113-110! Graham's 61-foot heave was the longest game-ending shot in the past 25 seasons, according to the NBA.

Hot Streak: Chicago's **DeMar DeRozan** had a historic hot streak in January and February. He had eight games in a row with 35 points, something that had been done by only six other players. However, in all of those games, he shot 50 percent or better from the field—THAT was an NBA first!

With this layup, LeBron James became the NBA's No. 2 all-time scorer.

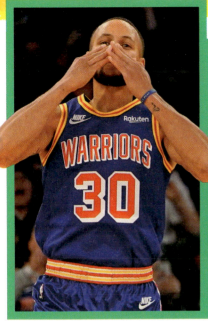

Mr. Three Pointer

Stephen Curry has been setting new standards for three-point success for years now. He was already the record-holder for a single season, with 402 in 2015–16. In a December game at Madison Square Garden, he buried his 2,974th career three-pointer. That pushed ahead of Ray Allen as the NBA's all-time leader. "I never wanted to call myself the greatest shooter until I got this record," Curry said after the game. "I'm comfortable saying that now." No argument here! The Golden State great finished the season with 3,117 career three-pointers.

Good Company:
Oklahoma City's **Josh Giddey** put up three straight games with a triple-double—at least ten each of points, assists, and rebounds. The only other rookie to do that was the great Hall of Famer **Oscar Robertson**, way back in 1961.

Quick Scoring:
Most players dream of putting in 50 points in a whole 48-minute NBA game. **Joel Embiid**, the 76ers superstar center, needed only 27 minutes! On his way to his first NBA scoring title, Embiid hit the half-century mark in a January win over the Magic. Philly was so far ahead, he played only a minute of the fourth quarter!

DeMar DeRozan

He's No. 1:
With the San Antonio Spurs' 26th win of the 2021–22 season, **Gregg "Pop" Popovich** became the all-time winningest coach in NBA history. The five-time NBA champ earned his 1,336th career win, passing **Don Nelson** for the top spot. As usual, the humble Pop credited his players and coaches instead of himself.

No. 2 and Rising:
Many fans think **LeBron James** is the No. 1 NBA player of all time. Well, after he dropped in a layup on March 19, he was one step closer to proving it. The basket gave him 36,929 points, good for second all-time. He passed **Karl Malone** and now has only **Kareem Abdul-Jabbar** ahead of him on the career scoring list.

NBA Playoffs

EARLY ROUNDS

➜ Congrats to these Play-In winners, as the NBA continues to tinker with the playoff format. Eight teams earned a spot in this mini-playoff. The Hawks, Pelicans, Nets, and Timberwolves all won to join the "regular" playoff teams.

➜ Golden State sent MVP **Nikola Jokić** and the Denver Nuggets home early, with **Stephen Curry** and **Klay Thompson** pouring in points.

➜ **Ja Morant** of Memphis continued his incredible season, lighting up the scoreboard and filling highlight videos during an amazing comeback to beat the Timberwolves.

➜ In wrapping up Phoenix's sweep of New Orleans, Suns' superstar **Chris Paul** was 14-for-14 in field goals. That was the best "perfect" single-game playoff performance ever.

➜ Philly's **Joel Embiid** was dominant in his team's win over Toronto. He poured in 45 points in one game, then hit a game-winning three in another.

Luka
Dončić

CONFERENCE SEMIFINALS

➡️ **Luka Dončić** put up massive points while leading Dallas to an upset series win over Phoenix. He is now third all-time for total points in his first 25 playoff games.

➡️ Boston rallied to win the final two games of its semifinal, knocking out two-time champ Milwaukee and superstar **Giannis Antetokounmpo**.

CONFERENCE FINALS

Eastern Conference
BOSTON 4, MIAMI 3
Both teams took turns blowing the opponent out for the first four games. Each held at least 20-point leads in their pair of wins. Miami forced a Game 7 by winning Game 6 in Boston, always a tough place to play. Miami superstar **Jimmy "Buckets" Butler** scored 35 points (he had 179 in the seven games!), but his final three-point shot missed, and Boston won.

Western Conference
GOLDEN STATE 4, DALLAS 1
The Warriors showed the Mavericks that a deep and talented team can overpower a superstar-led squad. Dallas did not give **Dončić** enough help. He scored at least 40 points in two of the games, but Dallas didn't win either one. **Stephen Curry** of the Warriors poured in the points, while

Kevon Looney emerged as a defensive and rebounding star for Golden State. Golden State returned to the NBA Finals for the first time since 2019.

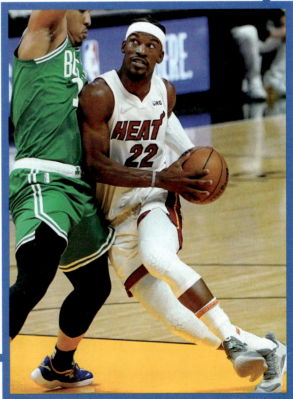
"Jimmy Buckets" nearly did it for Miami.

Veteran Al Horford finally reach the NBA Finals for the first time . . . but did not win.

NBA Finals

GAME 1
Boston 120, Golden State 108

At home for yet another NBA Finals, the Warriors looked strong. They were 9–0 in home games in this season's playoffs. **Stephen Curry** then set an NBA Finals record with 21 points in the first quarter. In the third quarter, Golden State outscored Boston 39-13 and took a 92-80 lead into the fourth quarter. Then the Celtics went on a 20-0 run. They poured in nine three-pointers, a Finals record for a final quarter. In storming back, they became the first team ever to trail in the fourth by 10 points and then win by 10 points.

GAME 2
Golden State 107, Boston 88

Remember Game 1? The Warriors did, and they borrowed a Celtics move to even the series. Golden State outscored Boston 35-14 in the third quarter, took a 23-point lead, and never let up on the gas. That was too much for Boston to overcome. Curry led the way with 29 points, while **Jordan Poole** contributed 17. **Jayson Tatum** had 28 to lead the Celtics.

GAME 3
Boston 116, Golden State 100

Led by **Jaylen Brown's** 27 points and Jayson Tatum's 26, the Celtics took a one-game lead in front of their extremely loud fans in Boston. **Marcus Smart** also had 24 as Boston's young trio outperformed Golden State's solo star, Curry, who still had 31 but did not get enough help. Warriors fans held their breath when Curry had to leave after a collision on the court. They hoped he'd be good to go for a key Game 4.

GAME 4
Golden State 107, Boston 97

Well . . . Curry was fine. In fact, he was more than that, pouring in 43 points to lead the Warriors to a series-tying win. He also had 10 rebounds for a historic double-double. He was the second-oldest player ever with a 40-10 in a Finals game. He also had 7 three-pointers. The Boston crowd did their best to get in his head, but he ignored them and the pain in his lower leg as the Warriors closed out the game on a 17-3 run. The series moved back to San Francisco for a huge Game 5.

GAME 5
Golden State 104, Boston 94

Curry didn't make a three-point basket for the first time in 233 straight games. Thank goodness the Warriors had **Andrew Wiggins**. The former No. 1 pick had 26 points and 13 boards. Thompson added 21. Poole made a near-half-court bank shot at the buzzer to end the third quarter. That spurred the Dubs to a 10-0 run to start the fourth and

26

Boston's **Al Horford**, in his first NBA Finals, scored a team-high 26 points in Game 1. He had played more NBA playoff games without making the Finals than any player in history!

they never looked back. Boston made 18 turnovers, which didn't help their cause.

GAME 6
Golden State 103, Boston 90

The Warriors won their fourth NBA title in eight seasons, while Curry earned his first NBA Finals MVP. The super-shooting guard had 34 points, plus 7 assists and 7 rebounds to lead the way, as he had throughout the playoffs. Golden State had a 21-0 run of points before the half that put the game away, although Boston made the end exciting, getting to within six at one point. When Curry hit his sixth three-pointer late in the game, he pointed to his fourth finger, where he would soon be putting his fourth NBA championship ring.

Stephen Curry

2021–22 NBA Awards

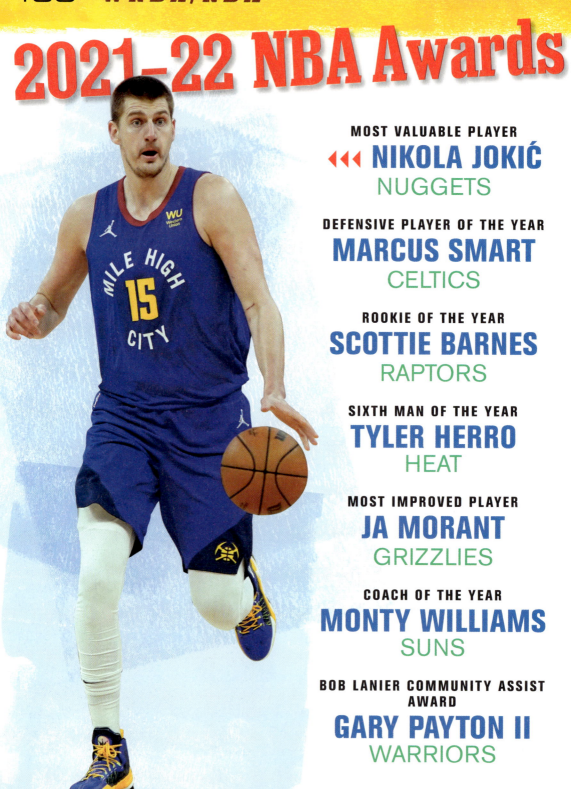

MOST VALUABLE PLAYER
◄◄◄ NIKOLA JOKIĆ
NUGGETS

DEFENSIVE PLAYER OF THE YEAR
MARCUS SMART
CELTICS

ROOKIE OF THE YEAR
SCOTTIE BARNES
RAPTORS

SIXTH MAN OF THE YEAR
TYLER HERRO
HEAT

MOST IMPROVED PLAYER
JA MORANT
GRIZZLIES

COACH OF THE YEAR
MONTY WILLIAMS
SUNS

BOB LANIER COMMUNITY ASSIST AWARD
GARY PAYTON II
WARRIORS

2021-22 Stat Leaders

30.6 POINTS PER GAME

Joel Embiid, 76ers

14.7 REBOUNDS PER GAME

Rudy Gobert, Jazz ▶▶▶

10.8 ASSISTS PER GAME

Chris Paul, Suns

2.0 STEALS PER GAME

Dejounte Murray, Spurs

2.3 BLOCKS PER GAME

Jaren Jackson Jr., Grizzlies

285 THREE-POINTERS

Stephen Curry, Warriors

71.3 FIELD-GOAL PCT.

Rudy Gobert, Jazz

92.5 FREE-THROW PCT.

Jordan Poole, Warriors

COLLEGE BASKETBALL

COMEBACK!

Favored to win, Kansas seemed shocked to find themselves down by 15 points at halftime of the championship game. North Carolina was shooting lights-out. But the Jayhawks rallied in the second half—big time! They set a record for the biggest comeback in title-game history and rebounded to win the school's fourth championship.

WIRE-TO-WIRE!
South Carolina started on top and—after a long and hard-fought season—ended up there! After losing in the final in 2021, the Gamecocks returned to change the story in 2022. Led by player of the year Aliyah Boston, they crushed Connecticut in the championship game.

2021-22 NCAA Hoops

High-scoring Caitlin Clark

The best part about the 2021–22 college basketball season was that there WAS a college basketball season. After more than two years of interruptions by COVID-19, most of this season was played . . . all the way to the thrilling ending!

As the merry-go-round atop the rankings showed (page 106), the sport was more balanced than ever on the men's side. Very few teams separated themselves from the pack. There were a total of five different No. 1 teams during the regular season, one of the highest totals ever. The NCAA tournament continued that theme. Fans were thrilled by some of the biggest upsets ever, along with a stack of lower-seeded teams advancing (even a shocking win by a 15 over a 2!). By the end, though, a group of very traditional powerhouse teams created a solid Final Four. One cool piece of trivia: All four teams had school colors of blue and white!

Duke was one of those teams. The Blue Devils had been in the news all season long because of their coach. **Mike Krzyzewski** (good thing they call him "Coach K") announced he would retire after the season. Coach K is one of the most successful hoops leaders ever, with five national titles and three Olympic gold championships. He led Duke to a thirteenth Final Four in 2022, setting a new record. As the season went along, he was honored by many opponents and fans. He didn't get title number six, but it was a great career.

On the women's side, the traditional powers stayed powerful. Defending champ Stanford had another great season, while Connecticut ended up in its incredible fourteenth Final Four in a row. South Carolina continued to grow as a national power, too. After winning it all in 2017 and finishing second in 2021, the team entered the tournament ranked No. 1 in the country. Superstar **Aliyah Boston** led the way this season with her powerful inside game. Meanwhile, Iowa's **Caitlin Clark** was lighting up the scoreboard. She seemed to be able to score from anywhere on the floor. Stanford's **Haley Jones** added Pac-12 player of the year honors to her lengthy list of awards; she helped the Cardinals reach the Final Four again.

For both the men and women, the NCAA Tournaments were, as usual, packed with great games. While the men's event included some shocking upsets and a No. 8 seed in the Final Four, the women's tournament settled down after some early surprises. Its Final Four included traditional powers—and a now-familiar champ!

After you check out highlights from the regular season, relive the great 2022 tournaments starting on page 108.

Oscar Tshiebwe

TOP AWARDS

WOODEN
Oscar Tshiebwe, KENTUCKY
Aliyah Boston, SOUTH CAROLINA

NAISMITH
Oscar Tshiebwe, KENTUCKY
Aliyah Boston, SOUTH CAROLINA

AP COACH OF THE YEAR
Tommy Lloyd, ARIZONA
Kim Mulkey, LSU

FINAL MEN'S TOP 10
ESPN/Coaches Poll

1. Kansas
2. North Carolina
3. Duke
4. Villanova
5. Gonzaga
6. Arizona
7. Houston
8. Arkansas
9. Baylor
10. Purdue

FINAL WOMEN'S TOP 10
ESPN/Coaches Poll

1. South Carolina
2. Connecticut
3. Stanford
4. Louisville
5. North Carolina State
6. Texas
7. Michigan
8. Iowa State
9. Maryland
10. Indiana

2021-22: Men's Notes

Logan Johnson of St. Mary's

Early Statement:
Gonzaga entered the season ranked No. 1. After a great Final Four run in 2021, UCLA was ranked No. 2. The two played in November in an early-season game. Gonzaga showed UCLA who was boss, beating the Bruins by 20 points! UCLA probably enjoyed the Zags losing, too, a few days later, when Duke beat Gonzaga.

Tough Week!
In mid-January, college basketball's rankings were scrambled. The Nos. 1, 3, and 5 teams all lost. No. 1 Baylor actually lost twice at home while top-ranked—the first time that had ever happened. They were beaten by Texas Tech and then Oklahoma State.

A New No. 1:
The first national basketball rankings came out in 1948. Auburn has been playing hoops all that time, but had never made it to the top spot. That changed when the Tigers beat Kentucky to continue a 15-game winning streak. With Gonzaga losing, Auburn moved into first place.

A Crazy Day:
Teams in the Top 10 will not look back on February 26 with any joy. For the first time ever, *seven* of the nation's top-10 ranked teams lost . . . on the same day! The biggest upset came when unranked Colorado shocked No. 2 Arizona. It was the highest-ranked team the Buffaloes had ever beaten! No. 1 Gonzaga lost to St. Mary's, but at least that team was ranked No. 23! No. 3 Auburn lost to No. 17 Tennessee, while No. 4 Purdue lost to fellow Big Ten team Michigan State. The Nos. 5, 6, and 9 teams also lost on that historic Saturday.

2021-22: Women's Notes

An Early Big Game: Women's basketball fans didn't have to wait long for a big game. In the season's first week, No. 1 South Carolina took on No. 2 (and 11-time national champion) Connecticut. The Gamecocks set the tone for the season with a powerful 73-57 win. **Elisa Pinzan** led the way with 26 points.

Streak Ends: UConn's tough luck continued in December when they lost to Georgia Tech. The game ended the Huskies' streak of 239 wins in a row against unranked opponents. A big reason for the L was an injury that kept Connecticut All-American Paige Brueckers out of the game.

New Scoring Record: Kansas State's **Ayoka Lee** scored 61 points in a win over Oklahoma, a new single-game women's NCAA Division 1 record. She topped the old mark by one point on her final basket, beating a record set in 1987 and tied in 2016. Lee set the record without a three-point shot; she used her size to push the ball through the lane for close-in shots. She was also nearly perfect from the free-throw line.

Lighting It Up: **Caitlin Clark** made some big scoring news, too. The Iowa sharpshooter became the first player—male or female—to have three games with 35 points and 10 assists in the same season. Clark also led her team to the Big Ten title. She also became the fastest player to reach 1,500 career points in the past 20 seasons!

Kentucky Surprise: **Dre'una Edwards** of Kentucky buried a long three-point shot with 4.2 seconds to shock South Carolina in the SEC Tournament final. You probably heard her shouting no matter where you were!

Ayoka Lee of Kansa State

Men's March Madness

St. Pete Shocker: Teams seeded No. 15 are not expected to win. In fact, they had won only 9 out of 135 previous games against No. 2 seeds. Make that 10! Tiny St. Peter's University shocked No. 2 Kentucky, a team many thought could be the national champ, 85-79 in overtime. It was the Peacocks' first-ever NCAA win. St. Peter's went on to make more history by becoming first No. 15 to make it to the Elite Eight. They beat Murray State and Purdue before losing to North Carolina. Their Cinderella story was one of the highlights of the sports year.

Gabe Kalscheur of Iowa State helped his team pull off a big upset over Wisconsin.

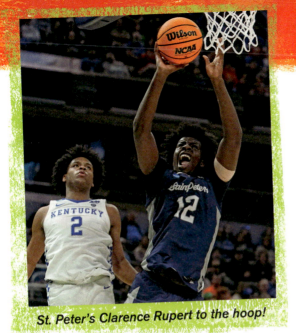

St. Peter's Clarence Rupert to the hoop!

12 over 5: It seems like it happens every year—a 12-seed beating a 5-seed. Fans filling out brackets always try to predict which it will be. This year, Richmond had the first of these "traditional" upsets, beating Iowa. Then New Mexico State topped Connecticut. Tradition!

UNC Holds Off Baylor: In the second round, the No. 8 North Carolina Tar Heels romped to a 25-point lead over No. 1 seed Baylor. But then top NC player **Brady Manek** was ejected for elbowing. Baylor was inspired and roared back to tie the game and force overtime. The Tar Heels were tougher in OT, however, and held on for a 93-86 upset win.

Comeback City: Iowa State finished the 2020-21 season with a 2–22 record. Talk about a turnaround.

After beating No. 6-seed Louisiana State, the Cyclones shocked No. 3-seed Wisconsin in the second round. The improvement was the best ever. No team with a winning percentage that low had ever won a tournament game the following season! They faced No. 10-seed Miami in the Sweet Sixteen, meaning at least one double-digit seed would be in the Elite Eight.

Regional Finals: After a tournament of upsets, the regional finals stuck to the seeds. All four of the higher-rated teams won their games, including No. 8-seed North Carolina ending St. Peter's miracle run. Villanova made it to their third Final Four in four seasons; they won it all in 2016 and 2018 (along with 1985, long ago!).

HOORAY!
Indiana cheerleaders saved the day during their team's game with St. Mary's. The cheerleaders used a lift move—**Nathan Paris** hoisted **Cassidy Cerny** up on his hands—to pull down a basketball that was stuck above the backboard. It was a great move, but Indiana's players didn't do as well and lost.

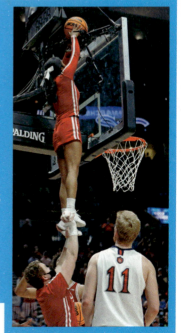

Men's Semifinals

North Carolina 81, Duke 77

"Instant classic" means a game so great and so memorable that we'll be talking about it for years. This was one of those games. These two schools are long and fierce rivals. They have played more than 250 times—but had never met in the NCAA tournament until this game. *And* it was Coach K's last game (see page 104). The game lived up to the hype. There were 18 lead changes as each team kept up the pressure. North Carolina's **Caleb Love** hit a long three-pointer with 25 seconds left to put the Tar Heels on top by four, and they held on for the dramatic win.

Kansas 81, Villanova 65

In a matchup of former national champs, Kansas poured in 13 three-pointers on the way to the win. Player of the year **Ochai Agbaji** was 6-for-7 on 3s by himself. The Jayhawks started out the game with a 10-0 run and never really looked back. 'Nova was missing key guard **Justin Moore**, and Kansas took advantage. Villanova got within six points late in the second half, but another strong run by Kansas sent the Jayhawks to the championship game for the tenth time.

Tar Heels fans "loved" this game-winning shot by Caleb Love.

National Championship Game

Kansas 72
North Carolina 69

If the semifinal that included North Carolina was an instant classic, this game was just a step or two behind. The Tar Heels roared out to a surprising early lead, burying threes and closing down the powerful Kansas offense. North Carolina scored 16 points in a row as the first half ended. At the break, UNC led by 15 points.

The Jayhawks regrouped at halftime in a big way. They started out the second half on a 31-10 run, erasing North Carolina's lead. But the Tar Heels came back, and the lead changed hands back and forth as the clock ticked down. With less than two minutes left, Kansas turned to its big man, **David McCormack** (right). The big center dropped in a baby hook to take the lead. A minute later, he missed on a similar shot, grabbed the rebound, and fought off two defenders to drop in the game's final points, putting KU up by three points. "When we had to have a basket, we went to Big Dave, and he delivered," said Kansas coach **Bill Self**.

North Carolina scrambled to make a tying three-pointer, but even semifinal hero **Caleb Love** could not find the bottom of the net. In fact, North Carolina didn't score at all for the last 90 seconds of the game.

Kansas guard **Ochai Agbaji** was named the Most Outstanding Player of the Final Four after his heroics in the semifinal and final. It was the fourth national championship for Kansas, to go with titles they won in 1952, 1988, and 2008.

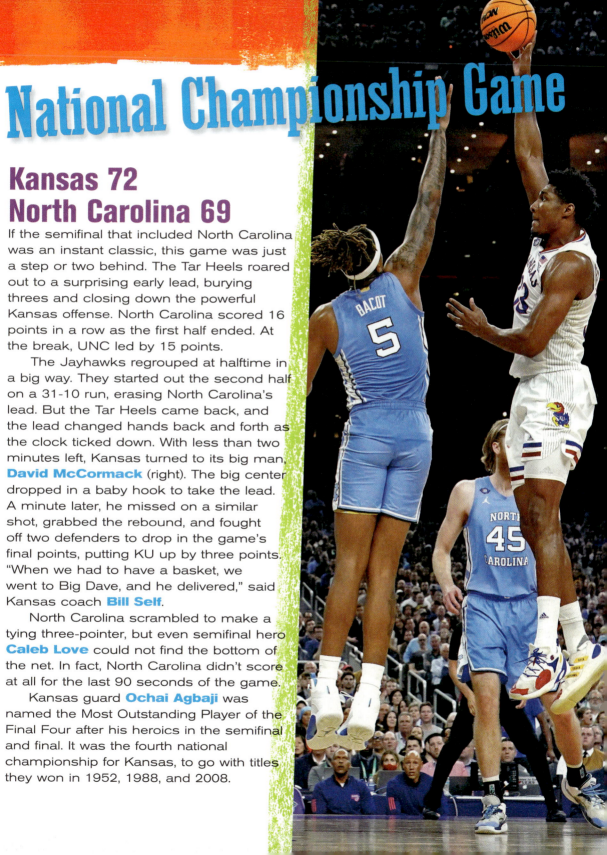

Women's March Madness

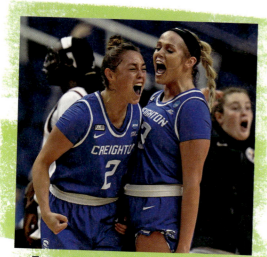

Tatum Rembao and Payton Brotzki

Up Then Down: Kentucky shocked No. 1-ranked South Carolina (page 107), but then stumbled in the first round of the tournament. Seeded No. 6, they were upset by 11-seed Princeton. It was only the third win by an Ivy League team in tournament history.

Dee-Fense! Dee-Fense!: South Carolina allowed a total of 54 points in its first two wins, over Howard and Miami. That's the fewest in those two rounds in tournament history!

12 vs. 5, Again: As in the men's tournament, the 12 vs. 5 matchup often ends with upsets. The 2022 tournament kept it rolling, as Belmont upset Oregon 73-70 in double overtime. A last-second shot by Oregon clanged off the rim to set off the Belmont celebration. Then No. 12 FGCU shocked No. 5 Virginia Tech, even though VT's **Elizabeth Kitley** had 42 points by herself!

Surprise Sweet Sixteens: Only two of the top 16 seeds did not make it out of the first two rounds. The first to fall was a real shocker. No. 2-seed Iowa, led by All-American super-scorer **Caitlin Clark**, lost to No. 10-seed Creighton 64-62 (left). The winning shot was made by **Lauren Jensen**, who had transferred to Creighton—from Iowa!

Bye-Bye Baylor: Another surprise Sweet Sixteen team was South Dakota State. Seeded No. 10, they upset Mississippi to face No. 2 Baylor. With a 61-47 win, SD State reached the school's first Sweet Sixteen.

Points Record: A 20-point scoring run by Notre Dame in the first period led to a school-record 108 points in their win over Oklahoma. The team put up 35 points in the first quarter; **Dara Mabrey** had five three-pointers. And never had a team won by as much as the Irish did in the second round—108-64 for a 44-point win. Also, in ND's earlier game, Olivia Miles became the first freshman ever—male or female—with an NCAA-tournament triple-double!

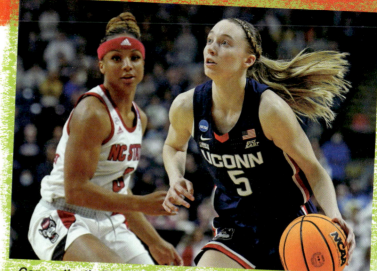

> **"Two days ago I said 'Win or go home,' but we won and I'm still going home. This is crazy. I'm just so excited no matter the location."**
>
> — **PAIGE BUECKERS**, ON THE CHANCE TO PLAY THE FINAL FOUR NEAR HER HOMETOWN IN MINNESOTA

Connecticut's Paige Bueckers led her team to the Final Four.

Boston Rocks: While leading South Carolina to a win over North Carolina, superstar **Aliyah Boston** had the game of a lifetime. She became the first player since 1972—male or female—with a 20-20 game while shooting 90 percent in free throws. Boston's 28 points and 22 rebounds led to a 69-61 win.

Dara Mabrey poured in points for ND.

Blue Jays Surprise: The biggest surprise of the women's tournament was No. 10-seed Creighton. By defeating Iowa State, they had tied the record for the lowest seeded team to reach a regional final. Unfortunately, there they ran into the South Carolina buzzsaw and a dream tournament ended with an 80-50 loss.

Classic Clash: The regional final between No. 2 Connecticut and No. 1 North Carolina State turned into one of the best games of the tournament. Both teams held the lead and looked ready to close it out, but both teams also staged solid comebacks. The game was tied after 40 minutes, and it took two overtimes before UConn wound up on top 91-87. **Paige Bueckers** scored 23 of her 27 points after halftime to lead the Huskies.

Women's Semifinals

Connecticut 63
Stanford 58

The Cardinals' defense of their 2021 title ended in a loss to a team that has won more national titles than any other. Connecticut was led by All-America **Paige Bueckers**, who had 14 points and 5 assists. A surprise was backup guard **Evina Westbrook**, who had 12 points coming off the bench. Connecticut will return to its first national-championship game in five seasons.

South Carolina 72
Louisville 59

Two No. 1 seeds met in this semifinal, but the championship game had room for only one. **Aliyah Boston** had a double-double—23 points and 18 rebounds—while controlling the lane on both ends of the floor. Four other players on her team reached double digits in scoring. On defense, South Carolina bottled up Louisville's star, **Hailey VanLith**, for only nine points after four games with at least 20.

National Championship Game

South Carolina 64
Connecticut 49

South Carolina was on a mission. In 2021, they lost in the championship game to Stanford. Superstar **Aliyah Boston** had missed a late basket that would have won the game. She was in tears afterward. She and her teammates vowed that 2022 would be different.

They started the season ranked No. 1 and that's how they ended it. Boston put her 2021 performance behind her and led her team to the 2022 national title. She dominated the boards, pulling down 16 rebounds, while scoring 11 points. Her teammate **Destanni Henderson** put in 26, the most she had ever scored in a game!

South Carolina got off to a strong start, building an 11-2 lead. They were ahead 22-8 after the first quarter. Connecticut was not hitting its three-point shots, missing the first eight the team took. However, led by star **Paige Bueckers**, Connecticut battled back and got within six points in the second half.

Henderson then scored a big three-point play and the Gamecocks never looked back. For Connecticut, this was the first time the Huskies had ever lost in a championship game. Under longtime coach **Geno Auriemma**, they had been 11–0. For South Carolina coach **Dawn Staley**, it was déjà vu: She earned her second national title leading the team. After the clock ticked to zero and the confetti flew, and as her teammates celebrated around her, Boston was in tears again—tears of joy.

Aliyah Boston dominated at both baskets for the champion South Carolina team.

NHL

STANLEY OOPS!

A dent in the bottom of the Stanley Cup? Well, yes. As Colorado Avalanche winger Nicolas Aube-Kubel skated toward his teammates with the Cup in hand for the team photo, he tripped and slammed the trophy on the ice. "I don't even know if they had it five minutes and there's a dent in the bottom already," said the Hockey Hall of Fame's keeper of the Cup, Phil Pritchard. The Avalanche earned the Cup with a big win over two-time champ Tampa Bay.

NHL 2021-22

Auston Matthews

The NHL finally returned to a regular 82-game schedule this season, and with so many games, there was plenty of scoring. The average goals per game was 6.3 (the most in 26 years), and eight players finished the season with 100 or more points. Six reached 100 for the first time, and four of those skaters were under age 26.

The league had to reschedule 105 games because of COVID-19 outbreaks, so NHL players could not take a break to play in the Winter Olympics. Instead, they used the time to score more goals! Toronto Maple Leafs' star **Auston Matthews** became the first 60-goal scorer since 2011–12, and Nashville Predators defenseman **Roman Josi** had 96 points, making him the highest-scoring defenseman in 29 years. Four players scored 50 or more goals, and 84 players combined to score 102 hat tricks. For the first time in NHL history, all eight playoff teams in a single conference

Kraken stars got stuffed salmon!

(the East) reached the 100-point mark.

In Seattle, the Kraken played their very first season. They finished at the bottom of the Pacific Division, but started a new tradition. When the top three stars were named at the end of each game, instead of throwing pucks into the crowd, they threw toy stuffed salmon (that's what the sea-monster Kraken loves to eat!).

At age 36, **Alexander Ovechkin** skated deeper into the record books with 50 goals, giving him a career total of 780. Only **Gordie Howe** (801) and **Wayne Gretzky** (894) have more—and Ovie is still playing.

And on April 29, the Dallas Stars let their emergency backup goalie, **Thomas Hodges**, play for the Anaheim Ducks after both Ducks goalies were injured. Hodges had to put down a hot dog and go to his car to get his goalie gear. In his first (and only) NHL game he stopped two of the three shots he faced; Dallas won the game. In real life Hodges is an insurance salesman and is almost blind in his left eye after a youth hockey accident. Just goes to show you: You never know what might happen at an NHL game! Read on to follow the 2022 Stanley Cup Playoffs and more!

2021–22 FINAL STANDINGS

EASTERN CONFERENCE

METROPOLITAN DIV.

HURRICANES	116
RANGERS	110
PENGUINS	103
CAPITALS	100
ISLANDERS	84
BLUE JACKETS	81
DEVILS	63
FLYERS	61

ATLANTIC DIVISION

PANTHERS	122
MAPLE LEAFS	115
LIGHTNING	110
BRUINS	107
SABRES	75
RED WINGS	74
SENATORS	73
CANADIENS	55

WESTERN CONFERENCE

CENTRAL DIVISION

AVALANCHE	119
WILD	113
BLUES	109
STARS	98
PREDATORS	97
JETS	89
BLACKHAWKS	68
COYOTES	57

PACIFIC DIVISION

FLAMES	111
OILERS	104
KINGS	99
GOLDEN KNIGHTS	94
CANUCKS	92
SHARKS	77
DUCKS	76
KRAKEN	60

Women to the Rink!

Before the puck even dropped for the January 13 game between the Los Angeles Kings and the Pittsburgh Penguins, trainer **Aisha Visram** made history. She became the second woman to serve behind an NHL bench. As the head athletic trainer for the Kings' AHL team, Visram was filling in for NHL trainers who were absent due to COVID-19.

About two weeks later, **Emilie Castonguay** was named assistant general manager of the Vancouver Canucks, where she was joined less than a month later by **Cammi Granato**. Counting all the coaches, scouts, and front office positions, there are now nearly 30 women executives on NHL teams and in the league's management.

In other cool diversity news, former longtime NHL winger **Mike Grier** joined the San Jose Sharks as the NHL's first Black general manager.

2022 NHL Playoffs

The Rangers celebrated sending Pittsburgh home.

There were plenty of surprises on the road to the Stanley Cup. Some teams that dominated in the regular season were knocked out in early rounds. A few underdogs did a lot better than expected. The excitement came early, with five of the eight first-round matchups needing seven games to decide a winner. When the Stanley Cup Final began in mid-June, fans were treated to a battle between a two-time champion and a hungry young team, in one of most exciting series in years!

➔ New York Rangers forward **Artemi Panarin**'s series-winning overtime goal capped a tremendous Rangers comeback. By knocking out the Pittsburgh Penguins, the Rangers became the first team in Stanley Cup playoff history to have three consecutive come-from-behind wins in the same series—while facing elimination in every game.

➔ The Florida Panthers had the NHL's best regular-season record and led the league in goal scoring. They had high hopes for their second-round matchup against their fellow Floridians, the Tampa Bay Lightning. Led by outstanding goalie **Andrei Vasilevskiy**, the Lightning turned the Panthers into pussycats. Tampa Bay swept Florida out of the playoffs and allowed them a total of only three goals in the whole series.

➔ The Calgary Flames and Edmonton Oilers revived their decades-old rivalry—called the Battle of Alberta—in a Wild West second-round matchup. The series opened with a 9-6 Flames victory. The Oilers had roared back from behind (6-2) to tie the game, but the Flames kept scoring. The 15 goals were the most ever in a playoff game between those two teams. The Oilers won in five games.

Western Conference Final

Colorado Avalanche 4, Edmonton Oilers 0

Two of the league's brilliant young stars, Colorado's **Cale Makar** and Edmonton's **Connor McDavid**, faced each other for the first time in the playoffs. The opener was a high-scoring game with Colorado racking up an 8-6 win. Colorado goalie **Pavel Francouz** closed the door with a Game 2 shutout, which he and his team then followed with a 4-2 win. Colorado forward **Artturi Lehkonen**'s overtime goal completed the sweep and sent the Avalanche to the Stanley Cup Final.

Eastern Conference Final

Tampa Bay Lighting 4, New York Rangers 2

The defending Stanley Cup champion Lightning were favored against the Rangers, who had come from behind in their first two series. The Rangers won the first game. Then they followed it with a 3-2 win! But experience took over as the veteran Lightning, led by captain **Steven Stamkos**, won the next four games and advanced to the Stanley Cup Final for the third season in a row.

Stamkos led his team back to to the Stanley Cup Final.

Stanley Cup Finals

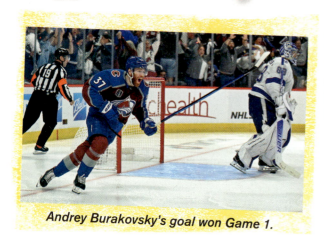

Andrey Burakovsky's goal won Game 1.

GAME 1
Colorado 4, Tampa Bay 3 (OT)

It was a dream series, with Tampa Bay making their third consecutive Final appearance, and Colorado reaching it for the first time in 20 years. Colorado roared to a 3-1 first-period lead, but late-second-period Tampa Bay goals tied the score. A scoreless third period, with goalie **Andrei Vasilevskiy** turning aside a dozen Colorado shots, set up overtime. Colorado's **Andrey Burakovsky** fired home the game-winner.

GAME 2
Colorado 7, Tampa Bay 0

Two goals each from **Valeri Nichushkin** and **Cale Makar** sparked Colorado to an overwhelming victory. Colorado goalie **Darcy Kuemper**, replacing an injured **Pavel Francouz**, turned away 16 shots to seal the commanding win. The win tied the NHL record for second-biggest shutout win in Stanley Cup Final history.

GAME 3
Tampa Bay 6, Colorado 2

Tampa Bay showed grit, with veterans **Ondrej Palat**, **Steven Stamkos**, **Corey Perry**, and **Pat Maroon** all scoring goals. **Nick Paul**, a late-season pickup by Tampa Bay, fired what proved to be the game-winner early in the second period, putting the Lightning back in the running.

GAME 4
Colorado 3, Tampa Bay 2 (OT)

Tampa Bay outshot Colorado 17-4 in the first period but managed to score only once. Colorado fired 17 shots in the second period but scored only once—a goal that Tampa Bay's **Victor Hedman** matched. Colorado tied it in the third, setting the stage for overtime—and a mystery. Colorado's **Nazim Kadri**, returning to the lineup after missing nearly three weeks due to surgery, cut in and snapped a shot past Vasilevskiy. The puck seemed to disappear, and nobody was sure what to do next. It turned out the puck was stuck in the top part of the net. Goal!

Where's the puck? Kadri slipped in a winner.

Colorado's Artturi Lehkonen (left) slides home the goal that clinched the Stanley Cup.

GAME 5
Tampa Bay 3, Colorado 2
Facing elimination, Tampa Bay's **Jan Rutta** opened the first-period scoring, but Nichushkin tied it with a second-period goal. The see-saw battle continued with goals by Tampa Bay's **Nikita Kucherov** and an equalizer by Makar. Tampa Bay's Palat blasted home the game-winner in the third to keep his team alive.

GAME 6
Colorado 2, Tampa Bay 1
Colorado carries the Cup! After an opening goal by Stamkos, Colorado tied it up thanks to **Nathan MacKinnon** and, on a wrist shot by **Artturi Lehkonen**, the game-winner. Makar won the Conn Smythe Trophy as playoff MVP, scoring eight goals and notching 21 assists. It was Colorado's first NHL title since 2001.

PLAYOFFS LEADERS

POINTS	**Connor McDavid**, Oilers, **33**
GOALS	**Nathan MacKinnon**, Avalanche, **13**; **Evander Kane**, Oilers, **13**
ASSISTS	**Leon Draisaitl**, Oilers, **25**
GOALS AGAINST AVERAGE	**Jordan Binnington**, Blues, **1.72**
SAVE PERCENTAGE	**Jake Oettinger**, Stars, **9.54**
POINTS BY DEFENSEMAN	**Cale Makar**, Avalanche, **29**

2022 NHL Awards

Makar led defensemen with 28 goals.

Hart Trophy
NHL MVP
Ted Lindsay Award
MVP (VOTED BY NHL PLAYERS)
AUSTON MATTHEWS, MAPLE LEAFS

Vezina Trophy
BEST GOALIE
IGOR SHESTERKIN, RANGERS

Norris Trophy
BEST DEFENSEMAN
CALE MAKAR, AVALANCHE

Calder Trophy
BEST ROOKIE
MORITZ SEIDER, RED WINGS

Art Ross Trophy
MOST REGULAR-SEASON POINTS
CONNOR MCDAVID, OILERS

Rocket Richard Trophy
MOST REGULAR-SEASON GOALS
AUSTON MATTHEWS, MAPLE LEAFS

Selke Trophy
BEST DEFENSIVE FORWARD
PATRICE BERGERON, BRUINS

Bill Masterton Trophy
PERSEVERANCE AND DEDICATION TO HOCKEY
CAREY PRICE, CANADIENS

Lady Byng Trophy
SPORTSMANSHIP
KYLE CONNOR, JETS

"[Former Red Wings star] Pavel Datsyuk was one of my heroes growing up. I tried to do everything he did. He won four Lady Byngs, so to see my name on the same trophy as him is pretty special." — KYLE CONNOR

NHL Stat Champs

123 POINTS
Connor McDavid, Oilers ▶▶▶

60 GOALS
Auston Matthews, Maple Leafs

85 ASSISTS
Jonathan Huberdeau, Panthers

96 POINTS (DEFENSE)
Roman Josi, Panthers

+64 PLUS-MINUS
Johnny Gaudreau, Flames

2.07 GOALS AGAINST AVG.

.935 SAVE PCT.
Igor Shesterkin, Rangers

9 SHUTOUTS
Jacob Markstrom, Flames

TIME FOR THE WORLD CUP
Thanks in part to Christian Pulisic's big goal against Mexico, the United States men's team earned a spot in the 2022 World Cup. As you read this, the Cup might be over, but we've got the story of how the Americans made it back to soccer's biggest show. Plus, read about European leagues, women's and men's pro soccer, and more.

SOCCER

NWSL 2021

Women's soccer continued to grow in popularity in 2021, but not without some battles off the field. The ninth NWSL season included some great matches—and a new champion—but the league was also in the news for some less-than-great reasons. The North Carolina Courage coach was accused of abusing players recently and in the past, and the coach was fired. As more news of this kind came out, the players protested. The league even stopped play for a few days to deal with the crisis. Eventually, it served as a signal that NWSL has to do a better job in working with its players, who got lots of support from the wider soccer and sports community.

On the field, the Challenge Cup, started in 2020, returned. The Portland Thorns FC won in penalty kicks, after an overtime tie with NJ/NY Gotham FC.

Portland used that hot start to post the league's best record, too.

The playoffs posted solid TV ratings and were played in packed stadiums as NWSL continued to grow into one of the biggest and best women's sports leagues in the world.

Semifinals
Chicago 2, Portland 0

On the road against the No. 1 team in the league, and the odds did not look good for Chicago. But the Red Stars played great defense and scored two long goals to earn an upset win. **Katie Johnson** and **Sarah Woldmoe** scored for Chicago. It will be the Red Stars' second visit to the NWSL title game.

Portland's team rushes for the goal after winning the Challenge Cup in penalty kicks.

US star Kelley O'Hara was clearly excited after scoring the winning goal in the NWSL final.

Washington 2, OL Reign 1

Washington fell behind in only the third minute on a goal by OL Reign's **Eugénie Le Sommer**. But they battled back to tie the game, thanks to **Trinity Rodman** (her dad is former NBA superstar Dennis Rodman!). The game was tight until the 68th minute, when **Ashley Sanchez** scored the go-ahead goal.

Final

Washington 2, Chicago 1 (OT)

When the Spirit needed a big goal, they called on a veteran. The score was tied after goals by **Rachel Hill** (Chicago) and **Andi Sullivan** (Washington). In overtime, defender **Kelley O'Hara**, a longtime member of the US Women's National Team, headed in her first goal of the season in the 97th minute. That broke the 1-1 tie and led to Washington's first-ever NWSL championship.

2021 NWSL AWARDS

MVP
Jess Fishlock
OL REIGN

GOLDEN BOOT (TOP SCORER)
Ashley Hatch
WASHINGTON

ROOKIE OF THE YEAR
Trinity Rodman
WASHINGTON

GOALKEEPER OF THE YEAR
Aubrey Bledsoe
WASHINGTON

DEFENDER OF THE YEAR
Caprice Dydasco
NJ/NY

MLS 2021

*Carles Gil,
New England*

A late start to the 2021 season due to COVID led to a wild finish that saw several teams lose playoff spots on the last day.

After starting in April instead of February, MLS roared through the summer with some great matches and rising stars. The New England Revolution were the biggest story of the regular season. They started hot, going 7–1–2 in their first ten matches, and stayed hot. By the end, they had set a new all-time record with 73 points and won the Supporters' Shield for the first time.

"Decision Day," as the season's final day is called, was a scramble. All the matches start at the same time, so every team needs to win without knowing what other teams are doing! In the East, DC United did its job with a win, but a Nashville–NY Red Bulls tie kept the United out. The Columbus Crew won the 2020 title, but missed the postseason.

Out west, the Los Angeles teams LAFC and the Galaxy both lost their games, and neither team won a playoff spot on Decision Day. Salt Lake, though, did squeak in on the final Sunday.

And 2021 was the final season for one of the best players in MLS history. **Chris Wondolowski** played 17 years, mostly for the San Jose Earthquakes. He scored a goal in their final match, giving him a career total of 171, by far the most in league history. He also saw action with the US men's team in his career, which ended with his retirement after that final goal.

Now read on to find out who ended up with the MLS Cup.

2021 MLS AWARDS

MVP
Carles Gil
NEW ENGLAND

DEFENDER OF THE YEAR
Walker Zimmerman
NASHVILLE

GOALKEEPER OF THE YEAR
Matt Turner
NEW ENGLAND

NEWCOMER OF THE YEAR
Cristian Arango
LAFC

COACH OF THE YEAR
Bruce Arena
NEW ENGLAND

MLS Cup
NYCFC 1, Portland 1
NYCFC win in PKs, 4-2

A wild MLS season ended in typically wild fashion in the rain in Portland. NYCFC continued its amazing run through the playoffs by scoring first on **Valentín Castellanos**'s first-half goal. The clock ticked down in the second half and the game was almost over when **Felipe Mora** kicked in a miracle goal in the fourth minute of stoppage time. The tie led to a penalty-kick shootout. NYCFC's goalie **Sean Johnson**, the game's MVP, stopped two PKs. Callens then put away the winning shot to set off the celebration of the club's first-ever MLS championship.

MLS Semifinals
NYCFC 2, Philadelphia 1

The Union roster was hit by COVID at the worst possible time. More than 10 key players were out for this game. Still, they got a break when NYCFC's **Alexander Callens** knocked in an own goal. However, New York tied the game minutes later on a goal by **Maxi Moralez**. With just two minutes left, **Talles Magno** won the game for NYCFC.

Portland 2, Real Salt Lake 0

The Timbers continued their great season with a shutout win over RSL. **Felipe Mora**, Portland's key player, gave them a great start with a fifth-minute goal. **Santiago Moreno** doubled the lead in the second half, and Salt Lake could not find the net. Portland heads to its third MLS Cup.

Johnson's PK stop helped his team win it all.

Champions League 2022

MEN'S

SEMIFINALS:

Spanish team Villareal came into the second leg of the semifinal against Liverpool trailing 2–0. Before halftime, they had tied it, and its home-field fans were hoping for more good news. They didn't get it. Liverpool scored three goals in the second half to swamp Villareal 5–2 over the two-game semifinal.

Manchester City took a 4-3 lead after the first game of their semifinal with Real Madrid. In the second game, they scored again to take a 5-3 overall lead. But the home Spanish team miraculously scored two goals in the final minute of play to tie the playoff. That led to a 30-minute extra-time period. Real got a penalty kick from **Karim Benzema** and held on to complete a shocking come-from-behind victory.

FINAL
Real Madrid 1, Liverpool 0

No team has won more Champions League titles than Real Madrid, and that stat stayed the same. The Spanish team won its 14th trophy in the world's biggest club competition. Brazilian star **Vinícius Júnior** scored the game's only goal in the second half. Madrid then hung on against an endless Liverpool attack. The man of the match was Real goalie **Thibaut Courtois** from Belgium. He made several brilliant saves to keep the net empty, diving for one save, while leaping to push another shot over the crossbar. Real Madrid really earned their championship: They had to beat Chelsea, Manchester United, and Paris-St. Germain on the way to the top.

Mohamed Salah, Liverpool

A sliding Vinícius Júnior of Real Madrid knocked in the only goal of the Champions League final.

WOMEN'S

FC Barcelona came into the Champions League final in May on an incredible streak. They had lost just once in the previous 41 games. They were a perfect 27–0 while winning the Spanish league. They had outscored their opponents, 197 goals to 16.

Along the way, they helped raise women's soccer to new heights. Their games against Real Madrid and Wolfsburg attracted more than 91,000 fans to their home stadium, setting new world records for women's league soccer. The team felt very confident heading into the Champions League final against Lyon from France.

But that's why they play the games—Lyon won 3-1, beating Barcelona for the second time in three years in Europe's biggest club event.

The win was historic. It gave the French club a new record of eight Champions League titles. After

Amandine Henry and **Ada Hegerberg** gave Lyon a 2-1 lead, **Catarina Macario** scored the third goal. She became the first American player to score in a Champions League final. Her teammate on the US national squad, **Lindsey Horan**, played a key midfield role.

Catarina Macario, Lyon

Super-sub Ilkay Gündogan smashed in this header to help Man City win the title.

2021-22 Premier League

Manchester City had won three of the previous four Premier League titles. And through most of the season, they looked like they'd repeat easily. But they stumbled in March and April, and Liverpool came on strong.

Man City looked like they'd be running away with it. In January, they were 13 points ahead. But over the second half of the season, Liverpool kept up the chase. With seven games left, the two teams were separated by only a point.

That was still Man City's lead when the final Sunday of the long season began. If Man City could beat Aston Villa, they'd be champs. But if they lost and Liverpool beat Wolves, then the men in red would hold the trophy.

Liverpool did its job, handily beating Wolves 3-1. **Sadio Mané** scored in the first half, while **Mohamed Salah**, who tied for the league lead in goals scored, added a second. **Andy Robertson** capped the scoring late in the game.

In a game being played at the exact same time, Man City was shocked to find itself behind 2-0 with less than 15 minutes left. No team had ever lost the Premier League lead on the final day. City kept that streak alive. The high-scoring team poured in three goals in less than five minutes to turn defeat into a 3-2 victory. **Ilkay Gündogan** scored twice, while **Rodri** pounded in a long goal. Liverpool fans could only watch the scoreboard in shock as the trophy slipped away.

Soccer World

TOP EUROPEAN LEAGUES

SPAIN: Nothing new here: Real Madrid won the league again for the 35th time. Yes, that's the all-time record for La Liga.

GERMANY: Bayern Munich is nearly as good as Madrid. Its title in 2022 was the 32nd for the famous club. They also set a record by winning their tenth straight.

FRANCE: Paris-St. Germain earned its tenth Ligue 1 title, tying a record set by two other clubs.

ITALY: AC Milan won its first Serie A championship since 2011 and snapped a streak of nine straight for Juventus.

AC Milan: Champs again

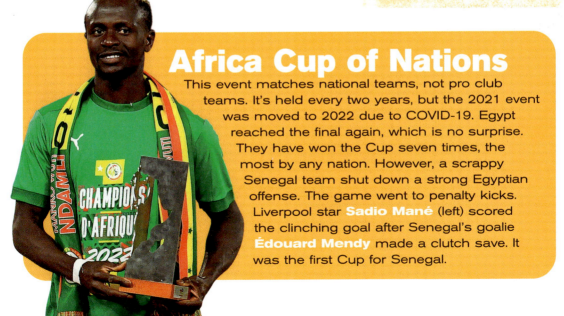

Africa Cup of Nations

This event matches national teams, not pro club teams. It's held every two years, but the 2021 event was moved to 2022 due to COVID-19. Egypt reached the final again, which is no surprise. They have won the Cup seven times, the most by any nation. However, a scrappy Senegal team shut down a strong Egyptian offense. The game went to penalty kicks. Liverpool star **Sadio Mané** (left) scored the clinching goal after Senegal's goalie **Édouard Mendy** made a clutch save. It was the first Cup for Senegal.

Women's Euro 2022

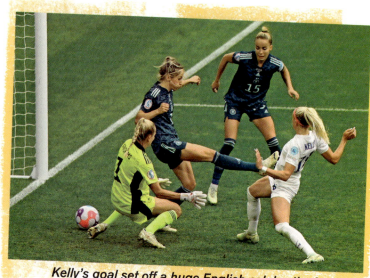

Kelly's goal set off a huge English celebration!

England is known as the birthplace of soccer, but no English team had won a major international title since the 1960s. That changed in July 2022 when the women's team captured the European Championship for the first time. Nearly 90,000 fans packed into Wembley Stadium in London to watch the final against Germany. The tournament was scheduled to end in Wembley anyway, so England got a big break by playing at home.

In the first semifinal, Germany's **Alexandra Popp** continued being a surprise star. Before the tournament, she was not expected to star, but ended up scoring six goals, including both in a 2-1 win over France. That gave her six for the tournament! In the other semi, England rolled over Sweden 4-0. The highlight was a backheel goal by **Alessia Russo** that went through the keeper's legs!

In the championship final, Germany scored late in the game to tie the score 1-1. With just ten minutes left in extra time, England's **Chloe Kelly** set off a nationwide celebration when she poked in a goal from short range. Soon after, **Prince William** handed captain **Leah Williamson** the coveted trophy as European champions—a first for England.

COPA AMERICA FEMENINA 2022

The South American championship of women's soccer came down to a tight final game. Brazil was highly favored, but Colombia had proven throughout the tournament to be a young team on the rise. The only goal of the match came late in the first half on a penalty kick. Brazil's **Debinha** (right) smacked it home, and then Brazil's defense was solid in the second half. As a mark of Colombia's success, forward **Linda Caicedo** was named the tournament MVP.

CONCACAF W Tournament

There was a lot on the line at this women's event for teams from North and Central America and the Caribbean. The winner would get an automatic spot in the 2024 Summer Olympics in Paris. The top four teams would earn spots in the 2023 World Cup as well. The United States team continued its dominant play, not allowing a single goal in five games. They beat Jamaica, Haiti, and Mexico in pool play, and then Costa Rica in the semifinal. In the championship game, the US defeated Canada 1-0, thanks to a penalty kick by **Alex Morgan**. It was a bit of revenge for the US, as Canada had knocked them out of the Olympics in 2021. The US, plus Canada, Jamaica, and Costa Rica, earned World Cup spots. Canada and Jamaica will play off for the other Olympic berth for CONCACAF.

Morgan buried the game-winning PK.

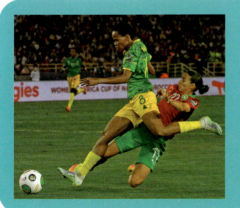

South Africa: "Finally!"

The South African team had reached the finals of the Women's Africa Cup of Nations four times . . . and lost four times. In 2022, they had another chance to capture the trophy, and this time they did it! With two goals by **Hildah Magaia** (left), South Africa beat Morocco 2-1. It was the first international title of any kind for the South Africa women's team.

US World Cup Qualifying

The United States men's team was shocked in 2018 when it lost the final qualifying game to Trinidad & Tobago. That loss knocked the team out of that year's World Cup. So it's been a long wait for another try to reach the world stage. The qualifying schedule of 14 games calls for stamina and strength. Other teams in the US's regional group, called CONCACAF, keep getting better, so the battle grows every four years. This time around, the US put together a solid run of key wins and earned a spot in the 2022 World Cup in Qatar, held in November and December because of that desert country's high summer heat. The qualifying matches were held in groups of two or three from September 2021 through March 2022. Here's how the US did on the road to Qatar.

US striker Ricardo Pepi

September 2021

A surprise scoreless tie with El Salvador got the US off on the road to Qatar. Then they tied 1-1 with Canada, who looked like a much-improved team. New US striker **Ricardo Pepi**, only 18 years old, scored a goal and had three assists in a big 4-1 win over Honduras.

October 2021

The US took a big step forward with a pair of wins—over Jamaica (2-0) and Costa Rica (2-1). The team lost 1-0 to Panama on the road for their first defeat of the qualifiers.

November 2021

Against their longtime rivals, Mexico, the US continued a yearlong win streak with a 2-0 win. Superstar **Christian Pulisic** came off the bench to score on a header in the 74th minute of a hard-fought game. **Weston McKennie** added a second goal late in the match. The result joined wins in Nations Cup and Gold Cup

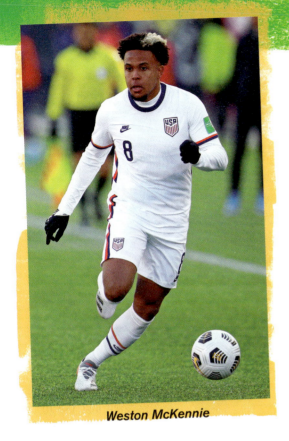

Weston McKennie

March 2022

Playing in Mexico is always very tough for the US team. They didn't score in this game, but then again, they kept the home team from scoring. The 0-0 tie gave the Americans a key point. A thumping 5-1 win over Panama, including a hat trick for Pulisic, meant that the US basically clinched a spot in Qatar. They only had to avoid losing by six goals in their final match: They did, falling only 2-0 to Costa Rica. The team was sorry to lose, but they ended up in third place in the CONCACAF group, and that was good enough to qualify, along with Canada and Mexico.

over Mexico. The US took a step back with a surprising 1-1 tie against Jamaica.

January/February 2022

The good news was a 1-0 US win over El Salvador, thanks to a goal by **Antonee Robinson**. The bad news was a 2-0 defeat to Canada. After five games, the Canadians were atop the CONCACAF standings, surprising many experts. **Cyle Larin** scored early, with **Sam Adekugbe** adding a second goal in stoppage time. It was only the second time since 1985 Canada had beaten the US team. However, the US bounced back with a 3-0 win over Honduras in February.

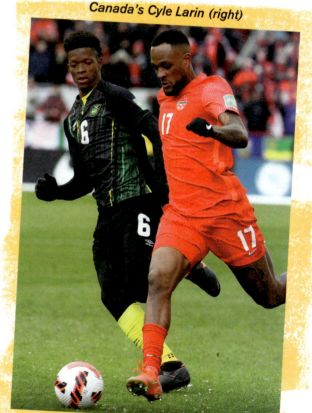

Canada's Cyle Larin (right)

2022 World Cup

For the first time, the World Cup was held in Qatar. The top 32 teams in the world sent their superstars to the desert country to try to bring home the biggest prize in soccer. Unfortunately, the event happened after we had to finish this book, so you know more than we do! But you can use these pages to keep track of the results.

On this page, fill in the final scores of the games played by the US team and the team from Canada. Let's hope you were able to include lots of victories!

On the right-hand page, circle the teams that advanced from the groups into the knockout stage. Then fill in the scores of the semifinals and the championship game. Did the team you expected win it all? Or was there a surprise winner?

US midfielder Gio Reyna

US World Cup Games

USA _____, Wales _____

USA _____, England _____

USA _____, Iran _____

OTHER GAMES:

_____

_____

_____

_____

Canada World Cup Games

Canada ____, Belgium ____

Canada ____, Croatia _____

Canada ____, Morocco _____

OTHER GAMES:

_____

_____

_____

_____

Group A

Ecuador
Netherlands
Qatar
Senegal

Group B

England
Iran
United States
Wales

Group C

Argentina
Mexico
Poland
Saudi Arabia

Group D

Australia
Denmark
France
Tunisia

Group E

Costa Rica
Germany
Japan
Spain

Group F

Belgium
Canada
Croatia
Morocco

Group G

Brazil
Cameroon
Serbia
Switzerland

Group H

Ghana
Korea Rep.
Portugal
Uruguay

SEMIFINALS

_____ _____ , _____ _____

_____ _____ , _____ _____

CHAMPIONSHIP GAME

_____ _____ , _____ _____

NO. 2 WAS NO. 1
The 2022 NASCAR season rocketed off to a
fast start at the Daytona 500. Austin Cindric
(2) zoomed past Bubba Wallace (23) to
capture his first NASCAR victory. It was also
Cindric's rookie season; the win meant he'll
challenge for the 2022 championship. In the
2021 season, another crop of superstars
battled hubcap to hubcap to find out who
would end up on top. Read about all the
action on the track in this section.

NASCAR

2021 NASCAR

The 2021 NASCAR season saw streaks and squeakers, wild rides, and wild races. Most importantly, it saw lots and lots of fans! Most tracks allowed fans back in, and folks responded by cheering their heroes through their masks!

Michael McDowell got the season off to a shocking start by winning his first Daytona 500 after a late-lap crash took out nearly a dozen cars. Then former Camping World Truck Series champ **Christopher Bell** showed he could handle a car, too, winning his first top-series win on the Daytona road course. Those two wins kicked off a busy start, as seven different drivers won the season's first seven races. Each earned a spot in the Chase for the Cup playoffs, which made the race tighter for the rest of the summer.

In March, **Kyle Larson** won the race in Las Vegas. Then he really turned on the gas. From May 30 through June 20, he won three straight races to leap into first place in the

Chase Elliott had all the right moves on the twisting track at Road America.

Ryan Blaney (12) squeaks past William Byron to win a tight race in Michigan.

season standings. Larson would have made it four in a row if not for a blown tire at Pocono's second race. He stayed in first place through August, adding another victory.

Chase Elliott was just waiting for a road course. In July at Road America, he got it and won his seventh career race on this type of twisting, no-bank track. He had a lot of work to do, starting from 34th place. He reeled in driver after driver and took the lead on the 46th of the 62-lap race. Though Elliott is only 25, his career road-track wins are third-most all-time in NASCAR history.

At the Michigan race on August 22, **Ryan Blaney** moved up in the Chase playoff standings with a super-tight win. He finished only 0.077 seconds ahead of **William Byron**. That is less time than it takes to blink!

As usual, the playoffs were packed with action (and even some controversy!) before the final four made it to the Championship Race. Follow along with all the big races and find out who was the 2021 winner on the following pages.

2021 Final Standings
Includes all Playoff drivers

PLACE/RACER	POINTS
1. **Kyle Larson**	5,040
2. **Martin Truex Jr.**	5,035
3. **Denny Hamlin**	5,034
4. **Chase Elliott**	5,032
5. **Kevin Harvick**	2,361
6. **Brad Kesolowski**	2,354
7. **Ryan Blaney**	2,350
8. **Joey Logano**	2,336
9. **Kyle Busch**	2,318
10. **William Byron**	2,306
11. **Kurt Busch**	2,297
12. **Christopher Bell**	2,279
13. **Tyler Reddick**	2,250
14. **Alex Bowman**	2,240
15. **Aric Almirola**	2,215
16. **Michael McDowell**	2,152

Denny Hamlin stayed in the hunt with his first 2021 win at Darlington.

2021 CHASE FOR THE CUP!

ROUND OF 16

DARLINGTON: Denny Hamlin picked a good time for his first win of the season. He finished ahead of **Kyle Larson** in this race to clinch a spot in the next round. He had entered the playoffs in seventh place, so he really needed the W.

RICHMOND: Hamlin almost made it two in a row, but he could not catch teammate **Martin Truex Jr.**, who won his fourth race of the season. He joined Hamlin in the next round. **Kyle Larson** also earned enough points to move on.

BRISTOL: Larson won this race, but he was already in, so the battle was for points to advance. Former champ **Kevin Harvick** survived a battle with **Chase Elliott** but both advanced. **Michael McDowell** started the season hot, winning the Daytona 500, but he was bumped from the playoffs.

William Byron's third-place finish gave him just enough to advance.

OUT: Aric Almirola, Kurt Busch, Michael McDowell, Tyler Reddick

ROUND OF 12

LAS VEGAS: This round started off like the last one, with Hamlin winning. He moved into the round of eight by holding off Elliott.

TALLADEGA: History was made at one of NASCAR's most historic tracks. When rain ended this race early, **Bubba Wallace** was in the lead and declared the winner. He was the first Black driver to win a top-level NASCAR race since 1963. Only a few Black drivers have ever taken part in the races, and the sport has been trying to encourage young racers to join. Wallace has been helping with that, and his win will surely aid the effort.

CHARLOTTE: Four more drivers saw their seasons end at the final race of this round. The biggest surprise of the quartet was Harvick. A 33rd-place finish ended the former champ's season. Larson won the race, but he was already qualified to move on. The final eight drivers headed on to Texas.

OUT: Christopher Bell, Alex Bowman, William Byron, Kevin Harvick

ROUND OF 8

TEXAS: Larson made it two in a row by dominating the race at Texas Motor Speedway. With the win, he became the first driver to clinch a spot in the final four to race in Phoenix with a shot at the season championship. He was the hottest driver in recent races, putting him in a good spot to bring home the Cup.

KANSAS: For the second time in 2021, Larson won three races in a row. No one had done that since 1987. With his spot in the finals set, the race was on for who would join him. Low finishes meant that former champs Hamlin, **Brad Kesolowski**, and Truex had to work hard in the next race to avoid being cut.

MARTINSVILLE: If the winner of this race was one of the final eight drivers, he would have automatically been in the final. That didn't happen. **Alex Bowman**, already eliminated, won in overtime. **Kyle Busch** finished second, but that left him three points out of the final four, which included Larson, Elliott, Hamlin, and Truex Jr. Hamlin made headlines after the race, too. He was so mad at Bowman for spinning him out late in the race that he blocked the race winner from doing his victory donut spin on the track! That set up some tense action in the championship race.

OUT: Ryan Blaney, Kyle Busch, Brad Kesolowski, Joey Logano

Wallace and his crewmates celebrated a historic victory.

"You always got to stick true to your path and not let the nonsense get to you. Stay strong. Stay humble. Stay hungry."

—BUBBA WALLACE

2021 Championship Race

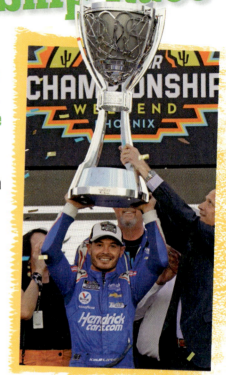

Only one person is inside a NASCAR vehicle, but the 2021 championship race proved more than ever that racing is a team sport. With about 30 laps to go, champ favorite **Kyle Larson** was fourth among the final four drivers aiming for the Cup. Then a yellow caution flag meant that all the teams could head to pit row. Larson's team rocketed through a four-tire pit stop in 11.8 seconds, their second-fastest of the year. As the cars sped back to the track, Larson had moved from fourth . . . to first! He stayed that way and held off **Martin Truex Jr.** to win his first NASCAR season championship. "Without my pit crew on the last stop, we would not be standing here," Larson said after the victory. "They are the true winners of this race. They are the true champions." The win in the race capped off a spectacular season for Larson that included a career-high 10 victories.

Teamwork in the pits—changing tires and pumping gas—made Larson a winner.

Other NASCAR Champs

XFINITY SERIES

Austin Cindric thought he had a repeat championship in the bag. He was leading late in the final race at Phoenix when a caution flag led to an overtime restart. **Daniel Hemric** zoomed up close to Cindric, then slightly bumped him as he rocketed past Cindric to finish in first place. That gave him his first Xfinity season championship. Incredibly, it was Hemric's first-ever race victory in NASCAR (out of 207 races). It capped off his best stretch of the season. He had five top-five finishes leading up to the big win in Phoenix. He could not have picked a better time!

Hemric had a flag-waving celebration!

TRUCK RACING

Sometimes finishing third is enough. In the season-sending battle in Phoenix, **Ben Rhodes** didn't need to win the race—he just needed to finish ahead of the other three playoff drivers, whose best finish spot was fifth. Rhodes passed into third place on lap 142 (out of 150) and held on to capture the big trophy. An early flat tire ended the chances of season points leader **John Hunter Nemechek**. The race itself was won from the pole by **Chandler Smith**, who was named the series rookie driver of the year.

Rhodes was on top after the last race.

WHAT A BATTLE!
A season-long race between longtime rivals Max Verstappen (left) and Lewis Hamilton thrilled Formula 1 fans in 2021. The two drivers traded victories and points. One of the best F1 seasons in years came down to the very final lap of the very final race!

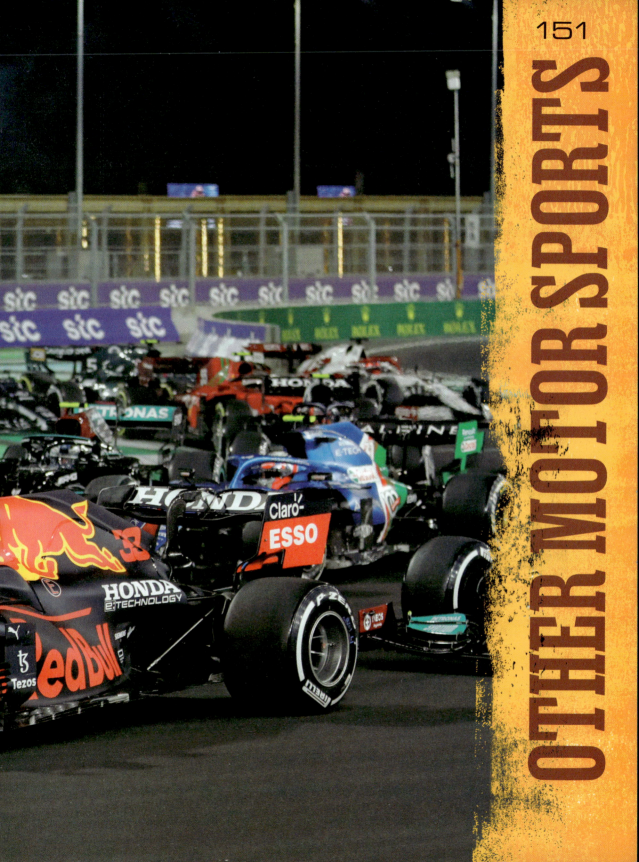

OTHER MOTOR SPORTS

The two best drivers . . . the last lap of the season . . . who will come out ahead?

2021 Formula 1

What more could racing fans ask for? The 2021 Formula 1 season came down to the last lap of the last race in the closest championship battle in decades. The final race ended in a shocking way, with a new champion crowned even as the old champion's fans grumbled.

How did it all happen? Formula 1 racing is always a duel among a small set of top drivers. Each race has 20 entries, but only a handful have the car and the driver to win. Throughout the 2021 season, the big duel was between seven-time champion **Lewis Hamilton** of Mercedes and rising star **Max Verstappen** of the Red Bull Racing team.

Hamilton won three of the first five events, but Verstappen won the other two. Thanks to a poor finish by Hamilton at Monaco, Verstappen actually led the series points race through May.

The Red Bull racer kept the pedal to the metal. By the end of June, Verstappen had won four races and led the points standings. He won three races in a row (France, Styria, Austria) to continue his fast pace, but Hamilton was slightly ahead in points as the season roared on.

In September, Verstappen used home cooking to retake the series lead. His

Max Verstappen

2021 F1 TOP FIVE

PLACE, DRIVER, COUNTRY	POINTS
1. **Max Verstappen**, Netherlands	395.5
2. **Lewis Hamilton**, Great Britain	387.5
3. **Valtteri Bottas**, Finland	226.0
4. **Sergio Pérez**, Mexico	190.0
5. **Carlos Sainz, Jr.**, Spain	164.5

win in the Netherlands Grand Prix vaulted him over Hamilton into first place. In Italy, Verstappen and Hamilton battled in more ways than one. In first and second place in the race, the pair collided, knocking both cars out. **Daniel Ricciardo** got his first win of the season after the crash.

The race in Russia was another key turning point. Unlike most types of racing, Formula 1 keeps the wheels turning even when it rains. Hamilton proved to be the master of the wet stuff by swerving ahead of his rivals to win. It was his 100th all-time race win, by far the most ever.

The lead kept changing, however. In Turkey, **Valtteri Bottas** won the race, but Verstappen's second-place points pushed him past Hamilton into the season lead. He doubled his lead with a victory at the US Grand Prix in Austin, Texas. Verstappen held off a charging Hamilton for his eighth victory of 2021. He added to his points lead with a dominating victory in Mexico. A highlight of that race was **Sergio Pérez**'s third-place finish. He was the first driver from Mexico to "podium" in that race.

The Brazil race showed why Hamilton remains the best driver ever in F1. A penalty forced him to start in the tenth row. No problem. By lap 40, he had made it into second place. Then, on lap 59, he roared past Verstappen to take the lead. After two more races, incredibly, the two were tied in points! There was one race left to determine the champ.

That race in the United Arab Emirates had an amazing finish. Verstappen started on the pole, but Hamilton swerved into the lead on the first lap. He kept pulling away and led

the Dutch driver by 16 seconds. Then, on lap 52 of the 58-lap race, another driver crashed. That forced all the drivers to slow down and stay in order . . . but meant that they bunched up. Just before the last lap, with the track finally clear of the crash, race organizers said the last lap would not be run at slow speed. Fans were shocked, and the Mercedes team complained loudly. "This is a motor race," the race director said in reply.

And they were off. Neck and neck to start, Verstappen pulled ahead in Turn 5 and held off Hamilton to win his first Formula 1 championship. It was a shocking end to a wild season, one F1 fans will never forget.

Verstappen took a quick quiet moment after his big win.

2021 IndyCar

The kids raced to the front as IndyCar got its 2021 season underway. Three of the first five races were won by young, first-time winners. Does this signal a new set of racing stars in the open-wheel circuit?

In Alabama, **Alex Palou** of Spain won his first race. In race number four at Texas, Mexico's **Pato O'Ward** came through the checkered flag. A week later on the road course at the famous Indianapolis Motor Speedway, **Rinus VeeKay** sped under the checkered flag. He joined two other drivers in early 2021 in winning their first IndyCar

race. All of them were part of a seven-race streak of races that each had a different winner.

Palou, however, had a pair of wins and four total top-three finishes by the end of June and led the standings.

At the Mid-Ohio race, American **Josef Newgarden** broke through for his first victory of the season as the points race tightened. That moved him into fourth place behind Palou, O'Ward, and **Scott Dixon**, setting up a furious chase for the title in the last months of the season.

At the Portland, Oregon, race in September, Palou moved ahead of O'Ward with a big victory.

Alex Palou kissed the championship trophy after the race at Long Beach.

INDY 500 '22

Marcus Ericsson was in the lead and on his way to his first Indy 500 win . . . when the race stopped with five laps to go. A crash closed the track while workers cleared the damage. When the cars restarted, they were bunched up again, and Ericsson had to hold off a charging back right on his heels! **Pato O'Ward** tried to pass Ericsson, but the Swedish driver held him off. A few moments later, he was enjoying the traditional jug of milk for the winner. It was only the second time a driver from Sweden has won this famous race.

With only two races remaining, it was a sprint to the finish. Then Palou came in second at Laguna Seca to extend his lead.

Palou became the first driver from Spain to win IndyCar when he finished fourth at Long Beach in the season's final race. **Colton Herta** won the event, while O'Ward finished 27th, which was not high enough to pass Palou.

The Spanish driver was excited for what his championship might mean back home. "It's going to open some eyes in Spain, and more people [are] going to discover IndyCar. They are going to fall in love with it. That's amazing. Exactly what we needed."

2021 INDYCAR TOP TEN

PLACE, DRIVER, COUNTRY	POINTS
1. **Alex Palou**, Spain	549
2. **Josef Newgarden**, USA	511
3. **Pato O'Ward**, Mexico	487
4. **Scott Dixon**, New Zealand	481
5. **Colton Herta**, USA	455
6. **Marcus Ericsson**, Sweden	435
7. **Graham Rahal**, USA	389
8. **Simon Pagenaud**, France	383
9. **Will Power**, Australia	357
10. **Alexander Rossi**, USA	332

Drag Racing

FUNNY CAR: This division came down to the wire. **Ron Capps** held the lead, but **Matt Hagan** was sneaking up behind him. At the final in Pomona, they raced each other in the second round. Hagan won, putting Capps' title in doubt. Then Hagan lost in the next round! He fell short by 37 points, and Capps earned the season championship, the second of his long career.

TOP FUEL: This high-powered division was not really in doubt. **Steve Torrence** dominated from start to finish. Of the season's first 19 events, he won ten! At the final in November at Pomona, all he had to do was finish top four to clinch the championship. That wasn't enough for Torrence, though. He powered past **Antron Brown** to win the event—his 11th in 2021—and the season Top Fuel championship for the fourth time in a row.

PRO STOCK: **Greg Anderson** already had four season championships in Pro Stock, but he had to wait a long time for his fifth. After winning No. 4 in 2010, he finally got No. 5 in 2021 with a terrific season. Anderson finished in the top three of every event except one, while winning four of them. In Pomona, he defeated **Erica Enders** in the semifinal to clinch the championship.

PRO STOCK MOTORCYCLE: Entering the final event, three racers each had a shot at winning this division. **Matt Smith** was in first, but he was chased by **Angelle Sampey** and **Steve Johnson**. Smith quickly leaped ahead in the opening rounds and never looked back. He piled up so many points, Sampey and Johnson could not catch up. Smith earned his fifth career Pro Stock Motorcycle title.

Steve Torrence steered his long, thin Top Fuel car to another season championship.

Motorcycle Racing

Dylan Ferrandis

2021 MOTOCROSS

With a week left in the 2021 season, **Dylan Ferrandis** of France wrapped up his first Motocross national championship in the 450 class. It was his first season in the sport's highest class! He won four of the first five events of the season and never finished worse than third in a race. Former champs **Eli Tomac** and **Ken Roczen** finished behind the rising star. Ferrandis was just the fourth rider to win the title in his first full season riding the bigger 450 machines. In the 250 class, another first-year rider, **Jett Lawrence**, took home top honors.

2022 SUPERCROSS

How do you win a season championship without riding in the final race? Be so far ahead that the last race doesn't matter! **Eli Tomac** piled up the points so high in AMA Supercross that when an injury kept him out of the Las Vegas final, he was already the champ. **Jason Anderson** won that race in Vegas, giving him seven victories in the season, including the final four in a row. But that was not enough to catch Tomac, who won seven races of his own, plus four other top-three finishes. Tomac earned his second Supercross title.

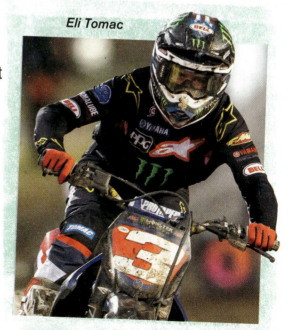
Eli Tomac

GOLF

LONG, TALL TEXAN
Scottie Scheffler is a 6-foot-3-inch Texan who hits the ball high and long and has a super putting touch. He finished a string of four wins in nine weeks in 2022 when he won the Masters for his first major championship. (See page 160.)

Catching Up on 2021

The second half of the 2021 golf calendar year featured some big news: After he was in a bad car accident, **Tiger Woods** helped coach the Ryder Cup instead of playing in it. An American won his first time out on an English course. And there was a huge comeback in the women's Evian Championship.

RYDER CUP

The first Ryder Cup since 2018—rescheduled from 2020 because of the COVID-19 pandemic—resulted in the biggest victory in 54 years for the United States. World No. 2 **Dustin Johnson** won all five of his matches to key the Americans' 19–9 win at Whistling Straits in Wisconsin. Johnson teamed with British Open champ **Collin Morikawa** for a win over Europe's **Paul Casey** and **Viktor Hovland** in an opening foursome match. The US closed that morning with a 3–1 lead and never looked back.

LPGA WINNERS

Down seven strokes in the final round, Australian golfer **Minjee Lee** didn't even think about winning the women's Evian Championship in France in July 2021. "I just tried to make as many birdies as I could," she said. She made enough to tie leader **Jeongeun Lee6**. Lee won on the first playoff hole. **Anna Nordqvist** of Sweden won the final major of the year, the Women's British Open, played in Scotland.

IMPRESSIVE DEBUT

Many American golfers need years of experience to get the hang of playing links golf. Links courses are in Great Britain and Ireland. They have coastal sand dunes, hard fairways, and high winds. But **Collin Morikawa** is not a typical American golfer. He won the British Open in the summer of 2021 on a links course in England.

Captain Steve Stricker (with trophy) and the US Ryder Cup team

2022 Men's Majors

The emergence of LIV Golf (see page 163) made 2022 a wild year in the sport. If anything, however, it meant even greater importance for the majors, which brought together all the world's best golfers on the same stage.

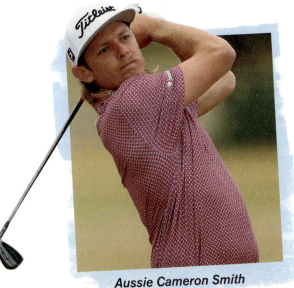

Aussie Cameron Smith

Rapid Rise

Scottie Scheffler capped an amazing two-month run with a three-shot victory over **Rory McIlroy** to win the Masters in April 2022. It was Scheffler's fourth win in nine weeks. The third win in that streak, at the World Golf Championships Match Play event in March, made him the world No. 1. He then proved it when he won at Augusta for his first major.

Sunday Charge

Justin Thomas roared from behind in the final round to win the PGA Championship in May 2022 for the second time. He came back from being seven shots behind on the back nine at Southern Hills Country Club in Tulsa, Oklahoma, on Sunday. A 65-foot birdie putt jump-started his comeback. Thomas made it to a playoff with **Will Zalatoris**, where he won it with a birdie on the third extra hole.

England Beats America

Before the US Open in June 2022, **Matt Fitzpatrick** had never won on the PGA Tour before. But he changed that at The Country Club near Boston with four solid rounds to become just the fourth Englishman in 100 years to win the US Open.

Aussie Run

Local fans were cheering for Northern Ireland's **Rory McIlroy** at the 150th British Open at St. Andrews, Scotland. He played really well but couldn't make enough putts on the final day. Instead, Australian **Cameron Smith** birdied six of the final nine holes and charged to victory with a final-round 64. McIlroy finished third.

MEN'S MAJOR CHAMPIONS 2022

MASTERS	**Scottie Scheffler**
PGA CHAMPIONSHIP	**Justin Thomas**
US OPEN	**Matt Fitzpatrick**
BRITISH OPEN	**Cameron Smith**

2022 Women's Majors

Golf's majors are all about tradition. And even though one of the sport's most fun traditions came to an end in 2022 (see below), the five women's majors continue to grow in fan interest, media attention . . . and prize money!

Last Splash
Jennifer Kupcho made a leap into Poppie's Pond in the spring of 2022. Each year, the winner of the Chevron Championship in Rancho Mirage, California, celebrated her victory with a leap into the water surrounding the 18th green. It was the final plunge, however, since the event will move to Texas in 2023.

Big Payday
Minjee Lee got the most out of the least at the US Women's Open in North Carolina in June. A record-low 271 earned her $1.8 million, a record for a women's tournament. It was the Aussie golfer's second victory in the last four majors.

Good Company
In Gee Chun won a major title for the third time in her career when she captured the 2022 Women's PGA Championship in Maryland. She joined stars **Inbee Park** (seven) and **Se Ri Pak** (five) as South Korean golfers to win three-plus majors in their career.

O, Canada!
At just 24, **Brooke Henderson** became the first Canadian golfer—woman or man—with multiple major titles in her career when she won the Evian Championship in France by one stroke in July 2022.

That's Kupcho in the middle, about to get wet!

WOMEN'S MAJOR CHAMPIONS 2022

CHEVRON CHAMPIONSHIP	**Jennifer Kupcho**
US WOMEN'S OPEN	**Minjee Lee**
WOMEN'S PGA CHAMPIONSHIP	**In Gee Chun**
EVIAN CHAMPIONSHIP	**Brooke Henderson**
WOMEN'S BRITISH OPEN	**Ashleigh Buhai**

Golf Notes 2022

A Long Time on Top

Twenty-three-year-old **Nellie Korda** set a record before she even placed a ball on a tee in 2022. That's because the Florida native entered the new LPGA season ranked No. 1 in the world. Korda became the first American woman to hold that post for a total of 26 weeks.

Korda: Top of the world!

55!

Andrew Ruthkoski posted that score—the lowest ever on a par-72 course—in 2022 at a Michigan course. He was going to play just a few holes for practice but started off eagle, birdie, birdie, eagle, eagle. Naturally, he had to keep going. Another eagle at nine closed a front-side 25. Six birdies on the back nine gave him his astounding 17-under-par total. He has his eye on the PGA Tour, so this is a great start!

One Ball . . . Two Holes-in-One!

Hole-in-one stories are always fun, and sometimes unbelievable. Here's one that's really amazing. In the spring of 2022, a 13-year-old named **Preston Miller** made a hole-in-one on the par-three, fourth hole of the Minneapolis Golf Club. Preston kept playing with the ball but lost it three holes later. **Ricardo Fernandez**, playing in a later group, found Preston's ball, teed it up on the par-three 16th, and put it into the hole. They discovered the coincidence in the clubhouse afterward. One ball, two holes-in-one!

Rare Double

What's rarer than a hole-in-one on the golf course? An albatross. That's a score of three-under-par on a hole. What's rarer than a hole-in-one and an albatross in the same round?

Almost nothing! According to *Golf Digest*, it's been done only 22 times. Australian golfer **Rowan McCarthy** pulled off the incredible feat at an event in London early in 2022. And he did it just four holes apart.

Big-hitting Bryson DeChambeau

LIV Golf

The biggest story in golf was about a rival to the PGA Tour. In the summer of 2022, LIV Golf signed away a stack of star golfers. Headed by former world No. 1 golfer **Greg Norman** and supported by money from Saudia Arabian backers, the new tour rattled the golf world. A big reason was objections to that Arab nation's record on human rights. Still, **Dustin Johnson**, **Phil Mickelson**, and **Bryson**

DeChambeau were among the big names who agreed to large money guarantees to jump to LIV Golf. In response, both the PGA and European golf tours banned any players who signed with LIV Golf from participating on their tours. If all the tours can't come together in the future, however, a complicated issue may have to be decided by the courts. Keep an eye on this one, golf fans!

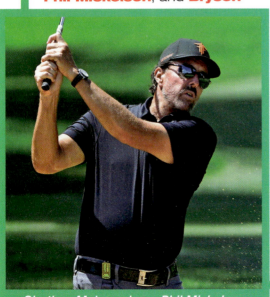

Six-time Majors winner Phil Mickelson

TENNIS

SHINGO SLAM
Shingo Kunieda exults after winning the men's singles final at Wimbledon in the wheelchair division in 2022. With the victory, Kunieda became the reigning champion at all four Grand Slam events. (See page 168.)

Catching Up on 2021

Almost History

With the summer of 2021 drawing to a close, Serbia's **Novak Djokovic** looked to make tennis history. He needed only to win the US Open to become the first man in 52 years to complete a Grand Slam: winning the singles title at all four major championships in the same calendar year. It was not to be. **Daniil Medvedev** beat Djokovic in the US Open final. That means **Rod Laver** (1969) remains the only men's player in the Open Era (post-1968) to win the Grand Slam.

Believe It

No one predicted **Emma Raducanu** winning the women's singles title at the 2021 US Open. Not even Raducanu! "Winning a grand slam—I can't believe it," the 18-year-old British tennis player said after defeating **Leylah Fernandez** of Canada in the final. Raducanu entered the tournament ranked No. 150 in the world and had to battle through pre-tournament qualifiers. No similar player had even reached the semifinals before. But in 10 rounds of play, Raducanu didn't lose a set.

Season Finales

The WTP Finals were back in 2021 after being sidelined by the COVID pandemic in '20. The event is a year-end tournament for the top eight women's players. Two of the three lowest-seeded players in the field, **Garbiñe Muguruza**

Surprise US Open winner Emma Raducanu

of Spain and **Anett Kontaveit** of Estonia, reached the '21 final in Mexico. Muguruza, a former world No. 1, was the crowd favorite all week. She even came out of the locker room wearing a Mexico soccer jersey. She rode the support of the fans to a straight-sets victory. Germany's **Alexander Zverev** had a pretty good year. He won the Olympic gold medal in Tokyo. Then he won the ATP Finals (the men's version of the WTP Finals) in Italy. That gave him six tournament wins in a busy year!

Women's 2022 Grand Slams

While the headlines at the men's majors have centered on the Big Three of Novak Djokovic, Roger Federer, and Rafael Nadal, the women have spread the wealth. Three different winners took the first three Grand Slam events of 2022.

Świątek won the French Open during a 37-match win streak.

Americans in Paris

Iga Świątek of Poland lost only one set the entire tournament. She routed **Coco Gauff** of the United States 6–1, 6–3 in the final to win her second French Open in three years. The good news for the future of US tennis is that three Americans reached the quarterfinals. In addition to Gauff, **Jessica Pegula** and **Sloane Stephens** reached the round of eight.

Tournament of Firsts

The Wimbledon Championships were played for the 135th time in 2022. It was a tournament of firsts. The first player from Kazakhstan won when **Elena Rybakina** defeated **Ons Jabeur** in three sets in the final. Jabeur's appearance in the final was a first, too. Tunisian-born Jabeur was the first Arab or African player to reach the final of a Grand Slam event.

On Top Down Under

Ash Barty became the first Australian in 44 years to win the Australian Open. The world's top-ranked women's player romped to victory in the tournament, winning every set in her seven matches. She beat the United States' **Danielle Collins** in the final. "That crowd the night of the final of the Australian Open was like nothing I've ever played in front of before," Barty would say later. "It was so much fun to enjoy that with them." The win gave Barty three Grand Slam titles to go with her 2019 French and 2021 Wimbledon wins.

2022 WOMEN'S GRAND SLAMS

AUSTRALIAN OPEN	**Ash Barty**
FRENCH OPEN	**Iga Świątek**
WIMBLEDON	**Elena Rybakina**
US OPEN	_____

Men's 2022 Grand Slams

Just like, well . . . like two tennis players trading shots back and forth, Rafael Nadal and Novak Djokovic battled through the men's Grand Slam season in 2022 for the top spot in the number of all-time majors titles.

A New All-Time Champ

Spain's **Rafael Nadal** took over the lead for most Grand Slam singles titles all-time with a dramatic win in Australia. **Novak Djokovic** and **Roger Federer** were unable to play, and Nadal took advantage. However, when he reached the final against Russia's **Daniil Medvedev**, he lost the first two sets. No one in the Open Era had ever won the Australian Open after doing that. But Nadal showed why he is the all-time champ by rallying to take the final three sets and the match.

Clay Court Master

No. 1—ranked Djokovic was back at the French Open, but he was no match for Nadal on the clay court in Paris—no player in the world is. Nadal beat Djokovic easily in the quarterfinals. He beat Norway's **Casper Ruud** in the final to claim his 22nd Grand Slam singles title. Of those wins, 14—another record—were at the French Open, where Nadal remained almost unbeatable.

Nadal celebrated Down Under!

2022 MEN'S GRAND SLAMS

AUSTRALIAN OPEN	**Rafael Nadal**
FRENCH OPEN	**Rafael Nadal**
WIMBLEDON	**Novak Djokovic**
US OPEN	_____

Close Behind

Before Nadal got too far ahead in the Grand Slam race, Djokovic pulled within one in July. He beat Australia's **Nick Kyrgios** to win Wimbledon for the fourth year in a row—and seventh in his amazing career. Djokovic set a record by appearing in his 32nd majors final, and by becoming the first player to win 80-plus career matches at the majors.

Tennis Notes

Kunieda created a new kind of "Slam"!

Two the Hard Way

This is the kind of thing that really needs to be seen to be believed—but we've got to tell you about it, anyway! In the spring of 2022, rising star **Carlos Alcaraz** and world No. 4 **Stefanos Tsitsipas** were playing in the fourth round of the Miami Open. Tsitsipas dropped a beautiful volley over Alcaraz's head that Alcaraz tracked well beyond the baseline. He returned the ball by hitting it through his legs, with his back facing the net. That shot arced over Tsitsipas's head, forcing him beyond the baseline to—you

Tsitsipas shows off a little tennis flair!

Shingo Slam

If you aren't familiar with the name **Shingo Kunieda**, you definitely should be. The Japanese star is the world's No. 1 wheelchair tennis player and has been as dominant in his division as **Novak Djokovic** or **Serena Williams** ever were.

In 2022, the 38-year-old finally won the only major championship that had eluded him: Wimbledon. He defeated Great Britain's **Alfie Hewett** for his 28th career major singles title—a record for any man or woman in tennis. The win also completed the career Grand Slam for Kunieda, who had already won the Australian Open (11 times), the French Open (eight times), and the US Open (eight times). And it also gave him the "Shingo Slam"—holding all four major titles at the same time, dating to the 2021 US Open.

Carlos Alcaraz is a rising star in world tennis.

years old. In May, one day after turning 19, Alcaraz stunned Nadal, his tennis idol, at the Madrid Open in his home country. The next day, Alcaraz beat world No. 1 Djokovic, too! Alcaraz went on to win the Madrid Open for his fourth title of '22 and had reached a world No. 6 ranking.

Surprise!

It wasn't a very big surprise that **Ash Barty** won the women's singles title at the 2022 Australian Open. After all, Barty was the top seed in the tournament. Instead, the big surprise came soon after. The world's No. 1–ranked women's player announced she was retiring from tennis because it was time to "chase other dreams."

Barty was only the second women's player to walk away while ranked No. 1. The first, **Justine Henin** of Belgium, was in 2008. Barty, who also had been a professional cricket player in her native Australia, first rose to No. 1 in the world in tennis in June 2019. Barty closed her terrific career by winning 25 of her last 26 matches. She was No. 1 in the world for 114 weeks in a row before retiring.

guessed it—return the ball by hitting it through *his* legs, also with his back facing the net. Alcaraz put that shot away to win the point (and eventually went on to win the match, and the tournament.) Look for it on video—it's wild!

Rising Star

Alcaraz, a teen sensation from Spain, continued his quick rise toward the top of the men's tennis rankings in 2022. He cracked the top 100 in the men's rankings in 2021, finishing the year at No. 32. Then he won three tournaments early in '22, while still only 18

CHAMPIONS

Here are the men and women with the most Grand Slam singles titles in the Open Era (since 1968, but not including the 2022 US Open):

MEN'S GRAND SLAMS		WOMEN'S GRAND SLAMS	
PLAYER	TITLES	PLAYER	TITLES
Rafael NADAL	22	Serena WILLIAMS	23
Novak DJOKOVIC	21	Steffi GRAF	22
Roger FEDERER	20	Chris EVERT	18
Pete SAMPRAS	14	Martina NAVRATILOVA	18
Bjorn BORG	11	Margaret COURT	11

A GOAT IN THE POOL
American superstar Katie Ledecky continued her climb to the top of swimming's all-time stars with another pile of medals at the 2022 World Swimming Championships. She won four gold medals, including one race by more than 14 seconds! Read more about Katie and other great athletes in this wide-ranging section.

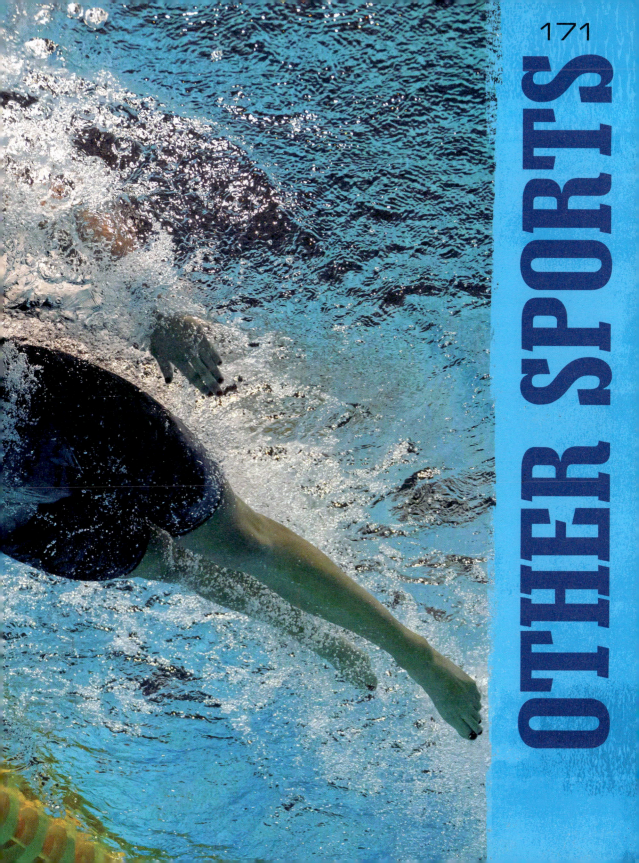

OTHER SPORTS

2022 World Athletics Championships

For the first time, the World Athletics Championships (the international term for track and field) were held in the United States. The site was Portland, Oregon, one of the runningest places in the country! The American team set a new record with 33 total medals, the most by one nation in the history of the event. Here are some highlights:

Chase Ealey powered her way to gold.

An American First

Chase Ealey went first in the women's shot put. And that's where she finished, too. Her opening throw of 67 feet, 2.75 inches proved to be the best of the competition. She became the first American woman to be a world champion in the event. In the men's shot put, it was an American sweep: **Ryan Crouser** won, followed by **Joe Kovacs**, and **Josh Awotunde**.

World Records (AGAIN!)

In the women's 400-meter hurdles, American **Sydney McLaughlin** had set a new world record twice in the past year. In the final in Oregon, she did it again. Her new time of 50.68 seconds was almost a second faster than the record she had set a few days

earlier. In the men's pole vault, Sweden's **Armand Duplantis** soared to a new record, too, reaching 20 feet, 8 inches (6.21 m) to break his old mark by 3 inches. On the final day, Nigeria's **Tobi Amusan** shocked fans with a 12.06-second world record in the women's 100-meter hurdles.

Speedy Americans

A trio of American sprinters won all the medals in the men's 100-meter race, something that had not been done in 31 years! **Fred Kerley** finished first with a time of 9.86 seconds. Just barely behind him were **Marvin Bracy** and **Trayvon Bromell**. Before the race, Kerley said, "If you ask me what I want to be, I want to be the Fastest Man in the World." Mission accomplished!

American men matched that sweep in the 200 meters. **Noah Lyles** set a new

Kerley celebrated after speeding to gold.

Felix wrapped up a golden career.

Goodbye to a Champ

Allyson Felix wrapped up one of the greatest careers in track-and-field history with a bronze in the 4x400-meter mixed relay. That gave Felix an all-time record of 19 medals at the World Championships. The super sprinter also won 11 Olympic medals, including 7 golds. She carried her daughter Cammy around the track after her final race. Wait! Un-retirement! Felix was called back to the meet a few days later to run a leg in the 4x400-meter relay qualifying. The US women won gold, so that makes Felix's record 20 medals!

Nice Run, Son!

Geoff Wightman has been announcing live track events for decades. In Oregon, though, he got the treat of a lifetime. He was on the mic when his son, British runner **Jake**, won the men's 1500-meter run in a huge upset over Norway's **Jakob Ingebrigtsen**.

Jake Wightman can't believe he's a champ!

American record with a time of 19.31 seconds. He was followed by **Kenny Bednarek** and **Erriyon Knighton**.

In the women's 4x100-meter relay, the US women's team pulled off a big upset. The Jamaican women's sprint team has dominated in recent years. But in an upset, the US team squeezed ahead of the favorites to win gold.

Athing Mu became the first US woman to win the 800 meters at the World Championships.

Late Sprint

When you have almost finished a race that is 10,000 meters long (more than six miles!), you'd probably be slowing down. At the Worlds, the racers in the women's event were sprinting! As the runners entered the final turn, they were running full out. **Letsenbet Gidey** of Ethiopia was the first over the line and won the half-hour-long race by less than a tenth of a second!

Winter X Games

A couple of weeks before the Winter Olympics (see page 18) began, winter athletes got to warm up a little bit at the annual Winter X Games, aimed at the more action-packed of the snowy sports. Here are some of the highlight performances.

Snowboard SuperPipe

Which gold medal would you prefer: Olympics or Winter X Games? Let's hope **Scotty James** answered X Games. He won his fourth gold medal in this event in Aspen, finishing ahead of brothers **Ayumu** and **Kaishu Hirano**. As you saw on page 28, Ayumu won the Olympic gold.

Teen Triumph

Kelly Sildaru won the Ski SuperPipe competition, but winning at the X Games is

Double-winner Tess Ledeux

It's another gold for superstar Sildaru!

A Good Day

Marcus Kleveland will remember January 22 as a pretty good day. First, he earned the silver medal in Snowboard Slopestyle. Then, he rocketed above the competition to win gold in the Big Air for a medal-filled day.

An Even Better Day

On the same day that Kleveland won two medals, so did **Tess Ledeux**. But both of hers were gold, which made her the first woman to win both Ski Big Air and Ski Slopestyle at the same Winter X Games. Take that, Marcus!

Great Ending

On the final run of the final event on the final day, **Nico Porteous** closed out the 2022 Winter X Games with a bang. He roared, soared, flew, and flashed down and above the halfpipe to win Ski Super Pipe gold for the second X Games in a row.

nothing new for the athlete from Estonia. She won her first title in 2016 and the 2022 medal gave her 10 for her career. Not bad for someone who didn't turn 20 until after the Games! She set a new record for the most career Winter X medals by any teenager.

A New Sport ... Sort of

This edition of the Winter X Games featured the first Snowboard Knuckle Huck event. Athletes flipped and spun after jumping off a shorter "knuckle," or very large hump in the hill. They were judged on how original and unique their jumps (or slides or hops or spins . . . there are no limits!) were, not on how well they repeated a particular trick. The winner, **Marcus Kleveland**, didn't get a medal, but he was awarded a set of brass knuckles on a chain.

Special Olympics USA 2022

While the Summer and Winter Olympics get all the headlines, the athletes of the Special Olympics might just be having more fun. This big sports event is held every four years for athletes with intellectual disabilities. The June 2022 event in Orlando, Florida, included more than 5,500 athletes from all 50 states taking part in 19 different sports. The athletes were put into "divisions" that matched similar sorts of challenges. Like the people who took part in the Summer and Winter Games, these athletes trained for months and years to reach the top of their sports. Here are some highlights from Special Olympics USA 2022.

Small but Mighty

The state of Vermont sent only six athletes to the 2022 Games...but half of them won medals! **Pascal Deppisch** came in first in his 1,500-meter event. He also earned bronze medals in two longer races. In her 25-yard freestyle swim, **Julie Bruner** brought home a silver medal. On the links, **Matthew Benn** was the silver medalist in the 9-hole golf event.

Practice Makes Gold

To get ready for playing flag football in Orlando, the team from Arizona got to practice in California's famous Rose Bowl. On the field where superstars from college and the NFL play, the athletes ran patterns and set up plays. Their hard work paid off when they won one of the gold medals at the Special Olympics.

More Than Medals

You just won a gold medal in volleyball. What are you going to do now? The Exceptional Foundation team from Alabama answered, "We're going to Disney World!" Actually, all the Special Olympics athletes got a tour of the Magic Kingdom. The team from Alabama had captured its first gold medal in the team sport and was ready to have a party!

Happy Homecoming

Tennessee's **Bethany Stineman** came home with gold medals in the shot put and the mini-javelin events. When she got back to little Nolensville, she was welcomed by the whole town! A police escort took her to her house, where a party with friends and neighbors was waiting.

HISTORY OF THE
SPECIAL OLYMPICS

In the early 1960s, **Eunice Kennedy Shriver**, the sister of President **John F. Kennedy**, ran a camp for kids with intellectual disabilities. One camp turned into many. As the movement grew, Shriver had the idea for an event to bring the active campers together. The first Special Olympics was held in 1968 in Chicago. Similar events are now held in every state, along with the USA games like the event in Orlando.

Rookie Win

Mary Borman from Arkansas says she had never tried stand up paddleboarding before she learned it was going to be part of the Special Olympics. So she tried it . . . and got good enough to win the gold medal in the 1,600-meter race.

Gold . . . Finally

Lousiana Special Olympian **Kirby Oertling** won silver in the pentathlon in 2014 and 2018. In 2022, he piled up enough points to finally reach the top in the five-event track-and-field competition that calls for running, jumping, and throwing skills.

What do you get when you win two gold medals? Bethany Stineman got a family party!

You'd shout, too, if you had just ridden Rich Strike to a huge upset in the Derby!

2022 Triple Crown

In horse racing, each horse is given odds—that is, what experts think are its chances to win. The higher the number, the "longer" the odds. So when **Rich Strike** was given odds of 80 to 1 to win the 2022 Kentucky Derby, that meant few thought he had a chance. But that's why they hold the races! In the second-biggest upset in the 148-year history of the Derby, Rich Strike won! In fact, the horse had only been added at the last minute when another horse dropped out. And he started farthest from the rail. But jockey **Sonny Leon** guided Rich Strike to a perfect ride . . . right into history!

Rich Strike's owners decided not to enter him into the Preakness, the second leg of the Triple Crown. That took a little bit of shine off the race, but **Early Voting** didn't care and took advantage, galloping to victory on a blazing hot day in Maryland.

The final leg of the Triple Crown is the Belmont Stakes. Rich Strike was in this race, and once again he was not favored. But there were no upsets this time. **Mo Donegal** was expected to win, and he did.

2022 Tour de France

The world's most famous bicycle race has a new champion. Denmark's **Jonas Vingegaard** knocked off two-time defending champion **Tadej Pogacar** of Slovenia. Vingegaard roared to the lead in the 11th stage of the 24-day, 2,067-mile race. It came during one of the Tour's many long, uphill climbs that test riders to the limit. Pogacar "cracked," as they say in cycling, and Vingegaard didn't. He held on through the remaining stages wearing the leader's yellow jersey. He celebrated with his family after the race ended in Paris. He also won the polka-dot jersey for being the top climber. It was the first Tour de France win for Vingegaard, who finished second in 2021.

Vingegaard got to the head of the pack in stage 11.

The Tour de France Femmes

That means the women's Tour de France, which was held in 2022 for the first time in 33 years! The final weekend of the eight-stage event saw a lot of drama. **Annemiek van Vleuten** was in eighth place on the second-to-last day. But she stormed up and over a mountain to grab the leader's spot. On the final day, she stayed 30 seconds ahead of second-place **Demi Vollering** and came home a champion.

Summer X Games

Here are some highlights from this annual extravaganza of action sports, held in 2022 at several Southern California locations.

Sky's the Limit

Not even 15 years old, **Sky Brown** is already a two-time X Games gold medalist! She won Skateboard Park for the second year in a row. Among the tricks in her winning run were a frontside 540, a backside lipslide, a nosegrab 540, and a frontside stale air. Skateboarders know what those are. Everyone else? Look 'em up!

Thanks, Pal!

What do you do if you're ready to ride in the X Games . . . and a thief steals all your gear? That's what happened to **Logan Martin**, but thanks to a friend who quickly came up with replacement gear, Martin swooped to his fourth gold medal in a row in BMX Park.

Welcome Back!

Skateboard Street Trick used to be an X Games regular event, but it was not held for 16 years until 2019. The new version of the event continued in 2022, and US athletes won all three medals. **Jamie Foy** led the way, followed by veteran **Nyjah Huston**, and **Dashawn Jordan**.

Turned to Gold

Momiji Nishiya of Japan won silver in Skateboard Street in 2019. In 2022, she finally made the jump to the top of the podium, after impressing judges with her wide variety

Winner Sky Brown with bronze finisher Kokona Hiraki

Winning Skate Vert for the fifth time took Jimmy Wilkins to new heights!

of . . . jumps (and other tricks). It was her first X Games gold. In the men's event, **Kieran Woolley** of Australia matched Nishiya as a first-time gold-medal winner.

Mr. Vert!

Jimmy Wilkins won his fifth Skate Vert Ramp gold in a row, the most ever by one athlete in this high-flying event. He amazed judges with a wild series of tricks, showing all of the experience that had brought him so many championships.

Magnifique!

In the Skateboard MegaPark event, a host of great skaters did their best moves on a new, super-sized Park course made just for this X Games. When the scores were final, France had earned its first-ever X Games skateboarding gold. "Bravo!" to **Edouard Damestoy**. He moved into the top spot on his fourth and final run!

Home Dirt

The Moto X and BMX Dirt events were all held at the Slayground, a huge course of dirt tracks, ramps, and hills built by rider **Axell Hodges**. So it was not surprising that Hodges was in the medal mix. After **Rob Adelberg** won Moto X Freestyle for his 14th X Games medal, Hodges got a silver in Best Whip behind **Julien Vanstippen**. Hodges got his gold in Moto X 110s on a course he can ride almost every day! Finishing just a foot below **Colby Raha** in High Air, Hodges took home his third medal of the day.

Medal King Tie!

Garrett Reynolds earned his 15th career X Games medal when he captured gold in the BMX Street event. That total ties him with skateboard and snowboard legend **Shaun White**. Reynolds won his first medal way back in 2008. Even more amazing, 13 of those 15 are golds!

Hungary's Kristof Milak thrilled fans in his home country with two gold medals.

World Swimming Championships

Held every two years in non-Olympic years, this competition is second only to the Games on the world swimming stage. As expected, American swimmers dominated, with Katie Ledecky (see box) leading the way. But athletes from around the world made their mark. Here are some of the highlights of the 2022 Worlds.

Mr. IM

France's **Leon Marchand** won gold medals in both the men's 200 and 400 individual medleys. In those races, swimmers do laps in each of the four main swimming strokes, so it takes real versatility and skill. Marchand's winning time in the 400 was the second-fastest all-time, behind only **Michael Phelps** of the United States.

A World Record—Backward

In the men's 100-meter backstroke, Italy's **Thomas Ceccon** shocked many experts by posting a world-record time of 51.06 seconds. He had done well before, but this was by far his best race ever—talk about good timing! Ceccon was later part of another shocker when his country won the men's 4x100-meter medley relay for the first time ever!

Hometown Hero

The championships were held in Budapest, Hungary, so fans were super-excited when Hungary's own **Kristof Milak** won the men's 200-meter butterfly for the second straight time, setting a new world record in the bargain! He later won the men's 100-meter butterfly, too.

Summer Swimmer

Canada's **Summer McIntosh** took home a pair of gold medals—the women's 200-meter butterfly and the women's 400-meter IM. Add in a silver in the women's 400 freestyle and she had a terrific meet. Not bad for anyone—but she's only 15 years old!

MEDAL RESULTS

	GOLD	SILVER	BRONZE	TOTAL
1. **USA**	18	14	17	**49**
2. **China**	18	2	8	**28**
3. **Italy**	9	7	6	**22**
4. **Australia**	6	9	4	**19**
5. **Canada**	3	5	6	**14**

King of the Pool

America's **Lily King** was already a world champion in the women's breaststroke as well as an Olympic winner. But she had never won at the 200-meter distance . . . until Hungary. She powered to a super-fast final lap, catching her competitors and winning by half a second.

Swimming's GOAT?

Is **Katie Ledecky** the best female swimmer ever? She certainly made her case at the Championships. After these latest Worlds—where she won four gold medals—she has 22 medals in this competition, an all-time record, including 14 golds. At the Summer Olympics, she has piled up seven golds and three other medals. She holds world records in the women's 800- and 1500-meter races (and she's the five-time world champ in the 800). Oh, and she also helped Stanford win two NCAA championships while setting dozens of college records. Wow!

Yes, the field is blue, and the Netherlands (in orange) dominated again.

Field Hockey World Cup

A familiar team won the women's world championship in this sport, which is more popular outside the United States. The top 16 teams (the US was not one of them!) gathered in the Netherlands and Spain to battle it out for the top spot. In the semifinals, the Netherlands squeaked past Australia in a battle of top teams. The Aussies had beaten the top-ranked Dutch team earlier in the tournament, but could not find the back of the net in this game. **Frédérique**

Matla scored the only goal. The other semifinal, between Germany and Argentina, saw more scoring. The two teams tied 2-2 after regular time. In the penalty shootout, Argentina won 4-2.

In the final, the Netherlands showed why they are ranked number one. They led 3-0 by the third quarter and never looked back. This was the third World Cup title in a row for the Dutch team and their ninth overall, the most by any nation in the women's event.

Lacrosse

2021 Premier League Lacrosse

The 2021 season was a big one for the Premier Lacrosse League. In only its third season, it merged with Major League Lacrosse in a unique way. Instead of having one team per city, the league traveled together and put on tournaments in a dozen major cities. Fans in lots of places saw lots of games! After a nine-week regular season, the championship game was in September 2021. Chaos LC outlasted Whipsnakes LC 14-9 to win the PLL title. **Dhane Smith**'s 18 playoff points were the most in 2021. Goalie **Blaze Riordan** showed why he had been named the winner of the Jim Brown MVP Award with a great game in the net. The PLL expanded to 10 weekends of games in 2022 and hopes to keep growing this popular sport.

2022 National Lacrosse League

The long wait for a championship paid off for the Colorado Mammoth. They won their first NLL title since 2006 by coming from behind to beat the Buffalo Bandits in a three-game series. In the clinching game—at the Bandits' home arena!—Colorado got spectacular play from goalie **Dillon Ward**. He set an NLL championship game record with 55 saves and was named the NLL Finals MVP. On offense, **Zed Williams** was the key for the Mammoth, scoring four goals and recording two assists. **Chris Wardle** topped that with five assists, while also scoring once. The final was an upset, as Buffalo had the NLL's best regular-season record.

Spot the ball? That's a goal for Colorado.

CHAMPIONS!

NFL

GAME	SEASON	RESULT
LVI	2021	**Los Angeles Rams** 23, **Cincinnati** 20
LV	2020	**Tampa Bay** 31, **Kansas City** 9
LIV	2019	**Kansas City** 31, **San Francisco** 20
LIII	2018	**New England** 13, **Los Angeles** 3
LII	2017	**Philadelphia** 41, **New England** 33
LI	2016	**New England** 34, **Atlanta** 28
50	2015	**Denver** 24, **Carolina** 10
XLIX	2014	**New England** 28, **Seattle** 24
XLVIII	2013	**Seattle** 43, **Denver** 8
XLVII	2012	**Baltimore** 34, **San Francisco** 31
XLVI	2011	**New York** 21, **New England** 17

Matthew Stafford led the Rams to the NFL title.

NFL MOST VALUABLE PLAYER

2021	**Aaron RODGERS**, Green Bay
2020	**Aaron RODGERS**, Green Bay
2019	**Lamar JACKSON**, Baltimore
2018	**Patrick MAHOMES**, Kansas City
2017	**Tom BRADY**, New England
2016	**Matt RYAN**, Atlanta
2015	**Cam NEWTON**, Carolina
2014	**Aaron RODGERS**, Green Bay
2013	**Peyton MANNING**, Denver
2012	**Adrian PETERSON**, Minnesota

COLLEGE FOOTBALL

2021 **ALABAMA**	2015 **ALABAMA**
2020 **ALABAMA**	2014 **OHIO STATE**
2019 **LSU**	2013 **FLORIDA ST.**
2018 **CLEMSON**	2012 **ALABAMA**
2017 **ALABAMA**	2011 **ALABAMA**
2016 **CLEMSON**	

Here's a handy guide to recent winners and champions of most of the major sports. They've all been celebrated in past editions of the YEAR IN SPORTS. But here they are all together again!

MLB

2021	Atlanta **BRAVES** 4, Houston **ASTROS** 2
2020	Los Angeles **DODGERS** 4, Tampa Bay **RAYS** 2
2019	Washington **NATIONALS** 4, Houston **ASTROS** 3
2018	Boston **RED SOX** 4, Los Angeles **DODGERS** 1
2017	Houston **ASTROS** 4, Los Angeles **DODGERS** 3
2016	Chicago **CUBS** 4, Cleveland **INDIANS** 3
2015	Kansas City **ROYALS** 4, New York **METS** 1
2014	San Francisco **GIANTS** 4, Kansas City **ROYALS** 3
2013	Boston **RED SOX** 4, St. Louis **CARDINALS** 2
2012	San Francisco **GIANTS** 4, Detroit **TIGERS** 0
2011	St. Louis **CARDINALS** 4, Texas **RANGERS** 3

MLB MOST VALUABLE PLAYER

Year	AL	NL
2021	SHOHEI **OHTANI**	BRYCE **HARPER**
2020	JOSÉ **ABREU**	FREDDIE **FREEMAN**
2019	MIKE **TROUT**	CODY **BELLINGER**
2018	MOOKIE **BETTS**	CHRISTIAN **YELICH**
2017	JOSÉ **ALTUVE**	GIANCARLO **STANTON**
2016	MIKE **TROUT**	KRIS **BRYANT**
2015	JOSH **DONALDSON**	BRYCE **HARPER**
2014	MIKE **TROUT**	CLAYTON **KERSHAW**
2013	MIGUEL **CABRERA**	ANDREW **MCCUTCHEN**
2012	MIGUEL **CABRERA**	BUSTER **POSEY**

COLLEGE BASKETBALL

YEAR	MEN'S	WOMEN'S
2022	**Kansas**	**S. Carolina**
2021	Baylor	Stanford
2020	**Not played**	**Not played**
2019	Virginia	Baylor
2018	**Villanova**	**Notre Dame**
2017	N. Carolina	S. Carolina
2016	**Villanova**	**Connecticut**
2015	Duke	Connecticut
2014	**Connecticut**	**Connecticut**
2013	Louisville	Connecticut
2012	**Kentucky**	**Baylor**
2011	Connecticut	Texas A&M

NHL

2022	**Avalanche 4,** Lightning 2
2021	**Lightning 4,** Knights 1
2020	**Lightning 4,** Stars 2
2019	**Blues 4,** Bruins 3
2018	**Capitals 4,** Golden Knights 1
2017	**Penguins 4,** Predators 2
2016	**Penguins 4,** Sharks 2
2015	**Blackhawks 4,** Lightning 2
2014	**Kings 4,** Rangers 1
2013	**Blackhawks 4,** Bruins 2
2012	**Kings 4,** Devils 2

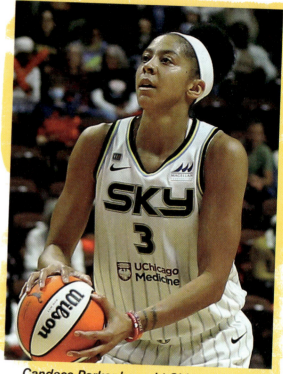

Candace Parker brought Chicago a title.

NBA

2022	**Golden State Warriors**
2021	**Milwaukee Bucks**
2020	**Los Angeles Lakers**
2019	**Toronto Raptors**
2018	**Golden State Warriors**
2017	**Golden State Warriors**
2016	**Cleveland Cavaliers**
2015	**Golden State Warriors**
2014	**San Antonio Spurs**
2013	**Miami Heat**
2012	**Miami Heat**

WNBA

2022	_____
2021	**Chicago Sky**
2020	**Seattle Storm**
2019	**Washington Mystics**
2018	**Seattle Storm**
2017	**Minnesota Lynx**
2016	**Los Angeles Sparks**
2015	**Minnesota Lynx**
2014	**Phoenix Mercury**
2013	**Minnesota Lynx**
2012	**Indiana Fever**

MLS

2021	New York City FC
2020	Columbus Crew
2019	Seattle Sounders
2018	Atlanta United FC
2017	Toronto FC
2016	Seattle Sounders
2015	Portland Timbers
2014	Los Angeles Galaxy

NWSL

2021	Washington Spirit
2020	Canceled
2019	North Carolina Courage
2018	North Carolina Courage
2017	Portland Thorns FC
2016	Western New York Flash
2015	FC Kansas City
2014	FC Kansas City

FIFA WORLD PLAYER OF THE YEAR*

Year	Men	Women
2021	Robert **Lewandowski**	Alexia **Putellas**
2020	Robert **Lewandowski**	Lucy **Bronze**
2019	Lionel **Messi**	Megan **Rapinoe**#
2018	Luka **Modrić**	**Marta**
2017	Cristiano **Ronaldo**	Lieke **Martens**
2016	Cristiano **Ronaldo**	Carli **Lloyd**#
2015	Lionel **Messi**	Carli **Lloyd**#
2014	Cristiano **Ronaldo**	Nadine **Kessler**
2013	Cristiano **Ronaldo**	Nadine **Angerer**
2012	Lionel **Messi**	Abby **Wambach**#

* was known as the FIFA Ballon d'Or [Golden Ball] from 2010-15.   # from the United States

PGA PLAYER OF THE YEAR

2021	Patrick **Cantlay**
2020	Dustin **Johnson**
2019	Brooks **Koepka**
2018	Brooks **Koepka**
2017	Justin **Thomas**
2016	Dustin **Johnson**
2015	Jordan **Spieth**
2014	Rory **McIlroy**
2013	Tiger **Woods**
2012	Rory **McIlroy**
2011	Luke **Donald**

LPGA PLAYER OF THE YEAR

2021	Jin Young **Ko**
2020	Sei Young **Kim**
2019	Jin Young **Ko**
2018	Ariya **Jutanugarn**
2017	Sung Hyun **Park** and So Yeon **Ryu**
2016	Ariya **Jutanugarn**
2015	Lydia **Ko**
2014	Stacy **Lewis**
2013	Inbee **Park**
2012	Stacy **Lewis**
2011	Yani **Tseng**

ATP PLAYER OF THE YEAR

2021	Novak **DJOKOVIC**
2020	Novak **DJOKOVIC**
2019	Rafael **NADAL**
2018	Novak **DJOKOVIC**
2017	Rafael **NADAL**
2016	Andy **MURRAY**
2015	Novak **DJOKOVIC**
2014	Novak **DJOKOVIC**
2013	Rafael **NADAL**
2012	Novak **DJOKOVIC**
2011	Novak **DJOKOVIC**

WTA PLAYER OF THE YEAR

2021	Ashleigh **BARTY**
2020	Sofia **KENIN**
2019	Ashleigh **BARTY**
2018	Simona **HALEP**
2017	Garbiñe **MUGURUZA**
2016	Angelique **KERBER**
2015	Serena **WILLIAMS**
2014	Serena **WILLIAMS**
2013	Serena **WILLIAMS**
2012	Serena **WILLIAMS**
2011	Serena **WILLIAMS**

NASCAR

2021	KYLE **LARSON**
2020	CHASE **ELLIOT**
2019	KYLE **BUSCH**
2018	JOEY **LOGANO**
2017	MARTIN **TRUEX JR.**
2016	JIMMIE **JOHNSON**
2015	KYLE **BUSCH**
2014	KEVIN **HARVICK**
2013	JIMMIE **JOHNSON**
2012	BRAD **KESELOWSKI**

INDYCAR

2021	ÁLEX **PALOU**
2020	SCOTT **DIXON**
2019	JOSEF **NEWGARDEN**
2018	SCOTT **DIXON**
2017	JOSEF **NEWGARDEN**
2016	SIMON **PAGENAUD**
2015	SCOTT **DIXON**
2014	WILL **POWER**
2013	SCOTT **DIXON**
2012	RYAN **HUNTER-REAY**

FORMULA 1

2021	MAX **VERSTAPPEN**
2020	LEWIS **HAMILTON**
2019	LEWIS **HAMILTON**
2018	LEWIS **HAMILTON**
2017	LEWIS **HAMILTON**
2016	NICO **ROSBERG**
2015	LEWIS **HAMILTON**
2014	LEWIS **HAMILTON**
2013	SEBASTIAN **VETTEL**
2012	SEBASTIAN **VETTEL**

DAYTONA 500 CHAMPIONS

2022	Austin **CINDRIC**
2021	Michael **MCDOWELL**
2020	Denny **HAMLIN**
2019	Denny **HAMLIN**
2018	Austin **DILLON**
2017	Kurt **BUSCH**
2016	Denny **HAMLIN**
2015	Joey **LOGANO**
2014	Dale **EARNHARDT JR.**
2013	Jimmie **JOHNSON**

INDY 500 CHAMPIONS

2022	Marcus **ERICSSON**
2021	Hélio **CASTRONEVES**
2020	Takuma **SATO**
2019	Simon **PAGENAUD**
2018	Will **POWER**
2017	Takuma **SATO**
2016	Alexander **ROSSI**
2015	Juan Pablo **MONTOYA**
2014	Ryan **HUNTER-REAY**
2013	Tony **KANAAN**

Larson celebrated with his son, Owen

Produced by Shoreline Publishing Group LLC

Santa Barbara, California
www.shorelinepublishing.com
President/Editorial Director: James Buckley, Jr.
Designed by Tom Carling, www.carlingdesign.com

The text for *Scholastic Year in Sports 2023* was written by **James Buckley, Jr.**
Other writers: **Jim Gigliotti** (Golf and Tennis); **Beth Adelman** and **Craig Zeichner** (NHL)
Fact-checking: **Matt Marini**.

Thanks to team captain Tiffany Colón, the photo squad of Emily Teresa and Marybeth Kavanagh, and the superstars at Scholastic for all their championship work! Photo research was done by the author.

Photography Credits